A WOMAN FOR OUR TIME

A WOMAN
FOR OUR TIME

the Servant of God
Mother Thecla Merlo

Co-Foundress of the Daughters of St. Paul

by
Spartaco Lucarini

translated by
the Daughters of St. Paul

St. Paul Editions

Approved by the
General Motherhouse,
Society of St. Paul, Rome,
n. 8468

Library of Congress Catalog Card Number 74—77253

Printed in U.S.A. by the Daughters of St. Paul
50 St. Paul's Ave., Boston, Ma. 02130

The Daughters of St. Paul are an international
religious congregation serving the Church with
the communications media.

CONTENTS

cathedral of the spirit, and I cannot but repeat the words of the German poet: "Mother Thecla knew how to create a magnificent cathedral out of her life because she possessed dogma. We, instead, have only opinions, and for this reason we no longer know how to produce similar masterpieces."

On what certitudes did Mother Thecla build the cathedral of her life? Mother Thecla entrusted herself to God; she entrusted herself to His Word; she staked her life on the Word of God.

The invitation that God presented to Abraham comes to mind: "Go forth from the land of your kinsfolk and from your father's house to a land that I will show you. I will make of you a great nation, and I will bless you; I will make your name great, so that you will be a blessing."

He believed in what the Lord said.

The entire existence of Mother Thecla was lived on this sublime, supernatural level, according to God's plan. Seen in this perspective, her life is something truly impressive and divine. St. John writes: "The power that has conquered the world is our faith," and Mother Thecla exemplified this throughout her life. She was able to build something wondrous, something solid, because she possessed certainty, she possessed immutable principles — just as God Himself is immutable.

This basis of faith was the force behind Mother Thecla's entire life — in particular, her charity. In her, the love that comes from God was truly maternal. Well-founded is the statement of the Founder to the sisters after her death: "You will still have many superiors, but in Mother Thecla you have lost a mother."

Today we speak much about community, fraternity, solidarity and communion of life. Without many words, Mother Thecla knew how to effect community. From her heart, from her charity, the community of the Daughters of St. Paul came forth.

Another fundamental point of Mother Thecla's life was a fortitude practiced to the utmost.

The Gospel tells us that only the violent will take heaven by force. Mother Thecla scaled the path to heaven by force. She adopted the principle of "violence" for herself, not others, and this "violence" had but one name — obedience. Mother Thecla was violent with the violence of Christ, who took the form of a slave becoming obedient even to death on a cross.

Just as at the basis of the Incarnation of the Son of God are His "Behold, I come to do the will of him who sent me" and the "Let it be done" of Mary, so at the base and foundation of the Daughters of St. Paul is the "Let it be done," the obedience, of this valiant woman. Faith, charity and obedience were the supporting pillars of Mother Thecla's virtue and holiness.

A person who had gone to Ars to visit the Curè was once asked, "What did you see there in Ars?"

He replied, "I saw God in a man."

If you were to ask me what I found in this life of Mother Thecla, I would have to give the same answer and add: "I have also seen that this woman is not dead, but that she lives in her daughters — the Daughters of St. Paul."

Reverend Sebastian Marchisio
Church of St. Damian, Alba

13

THE FRAIL SEAMSTRESS
OF CASTAGNITO D'ALBA

The "No" and "We'll See"
of Mama Vincenza

"I know your sister is a good seamstress. I could use her help in teaching a group of girls I've gathered together. Tell your mother to let her come."

This plea of the thirty-one-year-old priest startled the young seminarian, who stood there on the street listening in amazement. The place was Alba, in northern Italy. It was June, 1915.

Young Costanzo Merlo, who had a great esteem for that frail priest, with his intense gaze and ill-concealed dynamism, replied timidly,

"My sister wanted to enter the Sisters of Cottolengo, but they wouldn't accept her because she is anemic and her health is poor...."

"Tell your mother to let her come...," repeated the priest, paying little attention to the youth's comment.

As soon as he reached his home in the neighboring town of Castagnito d'Alba, Costanzo approached his mother. "You know," he began, "'the Theologian' would like Teresa to help him...."

Mama Vincenza Merlo was one of those practical women who want to see things clearly, with all their outlines and details.

15

Teach girls to sew?... A sewing shop run by a priest?... For what reason? After a little, she shook her head and said, as if to herself, "No, she's not going. I don't see clearly in this matter, because she can work right here at home."

The "No" was emphatic. It left no room for reply. Costanzo, the bearer of the strange request, knew his mother only too well.

Somewhat disappointed by the refusal, because he would have to tell the priest that his mission had met with failure, Costanzo began to formulate the reply he would give Father Alberione.... "Father, I told you it wouldn't be easy...."

To by-pass the obstacles and perhaps also to make up for his failure (could it be possible he had not succeeded in bringing about something that of necessity had to be good, since it was suggested by that holy man?) Costanzo approached Teresa herself one evening. His manner was half-mysterious, half-inviting. He was always outspoken with his older sister. Even though she often acted as a mother to him, he did not feel the same reverential awe for her that he felt for Mama Vincenza.

"Listen," he said, "'the Theologian' would like you to work with him...."

Teresa did not comment. As soon as she knew her mother had already given her "No," she did not feel it necessary to give her own answer. Within her, perhaps, she still nourished the hope that the Sisters of Cottolengo would accept her. She was disappointed at always finding herself held back by the poor health that continually kept her, more than all her brothers, under the watchful protection of her parents. However, from her parents Teresa learned to turn to God when things did not seem to go the right way, or at least, the way that is pleasing to us. Her other brothers, John and Charles, had learned this, too, as well as Costanzo, who had a certain kinship of religious inclinations with Teresa. Hence, that night Costanzo and Teresa decided to pray over the matter.

A few days later, very respectfully, Costanzo again broached the same subject to his mother. "Well, no, no. We'll see."

It was half a victory. When Mama Vincenza said, "We'll see," it was as if the wall had been battered down, at least to eye-level, so that one could glimpse what lay beyond.

Things went along quite smoothly after that providential "We'll see" — so smoothly, in fact, that one evening Teresa herself brought up the request of the Theologian of Alba. Taking all his courage in both hands, as he himself was later to say several times, her brother began to "plead her case," hoping that now success would smile on him and that he would receive not a sentence but an acquittal.

"Mama, you know that the Theologian is a really honest and good priest...."

This touched a soft spot in Mama Vincenza's heart. She had admired that priest ever since she had assisted at one of his Masses one Sunday morning.

"If he would like Teresa to help him," Costanzo continued, "it's a sure sign that he needs her and that she can really help him very much. Besides, Alba isn't too far from here. You can let her try it for fifteen days or so and then decide for yourself. I mean, if things work out, you can even let her stay until the fall. Otherwise, you can take her home. But, naturally, you do whatever you think best."

The last words faded out a bit shakily. Those that preceded them had been poured out quickly and daringly. He had sounded like a defense attorney rather than Mama Vincenza's son. When uttering his conclusion, instead, he had clearly recalled his position and perhaps feared to have said too much. After all, Mama Vincenza already knew how to do things. She didn't need so many explanations and proposals that were concrete down to the last details! To leave Teresa in Alba for fifteen days, to try it out.... But should a young man say such things to his mother? Didn't Mama Vincenza know how to raise children—she who had raised four? Could it be possible that she didn't know what was best for them?

Costanzo held his breath, inwardly reproving himself for having lacked all diplomacy and said too much.

Mama Vincenza bowed her head a little. It was a gesture that usually characterized her decision-making. "Yes, yes," she said almost at once. "We'll try. I'll accompany you myself!"

Costanzo felt as though he had just scaled the heights of Mount Blanc, even though until the day before, his friends had made fun of him. He looked at his mother and sister as if he were a great hero. He wanted very much to go immediately and tell Father Alberione how things had turned out. But Mama Vincenza had supper ready, and he sat down to eat with the others. Soon he would leave for the army, but Costanzo felt he had already conquered an enemy stronghold. He told himself he had completed his basic training.

Costanzo ate and drank heartily that night.

The Night Between Two Centuries

Mama Vincenza knew the Theologian well, both because of the fame this good priest had acquired and because of the sort of secret fascination inspired by his frail figure, which seemed to have the sole purpose of supporting the luminous face, with its penetrating, almost magnetic eyes.

Father James Alberione—"the Theologian"— was thirty-one years old at this time. He had already embarked upon an undertaking which to several had seemed risky and somewhat strange from the beginning—an extraordinary undertaking because it was being carried out by a priest. He, however, paid no heed to the critics; he paid attention only to being faithful to what he had promised God and himself— for a man of God he surely was, and on this point the critics found themselves disarmed. He had a will so persistent it could have shattered steel. A moment's conversation with him was enough to make one realize this.

His bishop, Most Reverend Francis Joseph Re, a man of unusual balance, orthodoxy and pastoral zeal, had appointed Father Alberione spiritual director of the seminary in Alba. At the time, he was only twenty-four years old. Then, at twenty-nine, Father Alberione had been appointed director of the diocesan newspaper, *Gazzetta d'Alba.*

A year after his ordination, this little priest had succeeded in obtaining a degree in theology from the Theological University of Genoa; this was why he was generally called "the Theologian." However, for Father Alberione, theology did not mean theoretical speculation as much as it meant practical application.

Even though modest and reserved, he was a man who lived fully the drama of his times. He knew only too well what was taking place in the arena of Italian cultural, social and religious life. He had firsthand experience with the anti-clericalism of the period right in his own district of Lange, and he knew that modernism was recruiting followers in many districts. To him, who had felt the call to the priestly vocation at the age of seven, the Church in that particular moment seemed to be suffering from the clash of the new and the traditional. Because the new ideas and customs were rapidly spread through the means of social communication, he believed that the same means could be used to propagate truth and good customs.

It was for this that he had offered himself to God while he was still a seminarian. That offering had taken place on the memorable "night between two centuries" during a nocturnal vigil anticipating 1901. He had prayed as his heart directed him, "Yes, Lord, I want to do something for You and for the men of the new century!" His prayer had been raised with the hope that there would be a renewal, a new impetus in Christian life; that there would be new apostles preaching the Gospel message in a manner adapted to the times, proclaiming it in an age menaced by a rebirth of materialism and practical paganism.

The memory of that night never left him: he thought of one project after another, waiting for the proper moment to make each of them a reality.

In the meantime, as a young priest, carrying out his ministry, he had the opportunity to become familiar with the people of various towns around Alba: Cherasco, Narzole, Benevello.... When the people heard him speak, they agreed at once that he was consumed by a desire to proclaim the Word. His preaching, not at all loud or fiery, penetrated into souls, tore down, built up, and worked the wonder of rousing up vocations. It was from the depths of his own soul that he communicated this fever that consumed him.

But a fever also consumed his body. In fact, while he was spiritual director of the seminary in Alba, it took little to realize that tuberculosis had already attacked the frail body that subjected itself to a continual struggle. There were those who hinted that his vocation was a waste because he could not have many years left. At that time tuberculosis was not an illness of little account, if it is today. Certainly, there was hardly enough physical strength for the things that he intended to accomplish.

But the will sustained everything. If he wanted to live, it was assurance enough that he would pull through. And that was exactly what happened. He lived to be eighty-seven and died in 1971, after founding and sustaining up to eight religious institutes and leaving behind more than 6,000 consecrated persons all over the world proclaiming the Christian message through the most modern means of social communication: press, films, radio, records, television.

Teresa's "Yes"

The next Sunday morning, keeping the promise that she had made, Mama Vincenza presented Teresa to the Theologian in the Church of St. Damian in Alba. She left Teresa in the pew to pray, for she wanted to speak to the priest first herself. Father Alberione had to be well aware that her daughter had come with her consent. Mama Vincenza would emphasize such details even in words. It was also important for Teresa to know that her mother had spoken with Father Alberione first.

What the priest said to Mama Vincenza will never be known. From what her daughter said later, as we shall see, it might be concluded that they spoke in very general terms — the priest limiting himself only to listening to the mother's views on her daughter's health, religious inclinations and the communities that she would have chosen to join. However, we can only conjecture as to what actually occurred.

Instead we have from Teresa's own lips an account of her own meeting with the Theologian. Here it is: "He knew I was a seamstress. He said that I would work in the sewing shop that he had opened in Piazza Cherasca in Alba. 'For now there is sewing to be done,' he said, 'but later there will be printing, and furthermore a Congregation of sisters working with the good press.... If you wish, let's go and see...."

Teresa added,

"With me was my mother, who had accompanied me from Castagnito to Alba. She decided to let me stay there fifteen days so I could see how things were."

Mama Vincenza had kept her promise, and now she accepted all the consequences.

Not from Teresa, who toned down her account of the conversation, but from other confidences, we learn that her first meeting with Father Alberione was not just a simple conversation or an ordinary exchange of views. It was one of those encounters in which divine Providence lies in wait for a soul and forcefully inclines it to respond and act in a particular way.

Father Alberione also spoke of this meeting later on, and he confessed: "When I invited her to begin, I said, 'For the love of God!' And this was enough to persuade her; she needed no other motives."

Father Alberione confided to someone that he had also prayed before that encounter.

That something exceptional had taken place did not escape Mama Vincenza, for there was something decisive about Teresa's gaze and step as she came out of church.

The mother anxiously tried to ask what the Theologian had wanted. And Teresa told her about the sewing shop, the good press and the period of trying it out.

"But, you, what did you answer?"

"I told him, 'Yes!'"

A new chapter was beginning in the life of Teresa Merlo.

"I Wanted Him To Be a Priest So He Would Work Hard"

They were a sound family — the Merlos. With four children, born within a period of six years, problems were not lacking, especially when the land did not yield in proportion to the work that it required.

Today, there are no more than nine hundred inhabitants in Castagnito, if there are that many. For now people make their way down out of the hills where the town is situated, on the left bank of the Tanaro River, between Alba and Asti, in the region called "Astisio." Back then, instead, people really had to struggle; the times were hard, and the mouths were many.

Maria Teresa, the second child, was born on February 20, 1894, and was baptized two days later by the Reverend Pietro Palladino. Those who knew her during her early years say she was a very beautiful child. She had lovely eyes and a penetrating gaze that she always retained. She was intelligent and lively. But she was also frail, very frail, and needed much care.

Her paternal grandmother foresaw that despite her physical frailty the child would accomplish great things in life. Don't ask the elderly why they have presentiments of this kind. They simply have them, that's all.

On her deathbed, therefore, Teresa's grandmother turned to her daughter-in-law and said simply, "I recommend this little one to you in a particular way, because she must do much good with her life. Take care of her." Even though said so casually, it was like a solemn trust. Mama Vincenza had not needed such a recommendation, for the upbringing of her children was something she had in her very blood. She began to train and guide them, from the time she was nursing them, with an educational skill made up of little theory but much good sense and practical lessons—a skill that was certainly inherited from her own mother.

When already a pastor in Barolo, her priest-son, Costanzo Leone, described Mama Vincenza with these bold strokes:

"My mother was well-known in the town as a practicing religious woman, but above all, as a hardworking, conscientious and exemplary mother. The education of her children was for her a mission which she carried out uprightly and decisively. She was inflexible when it came to keeping away from the family not only what was evil, but even what was less perfect."

That her upright life, committed to the good, was not an exterior attitude, but arose from a profound conviction, was shown among other things in many incidents of her life, which her family recalls in abundance.

Mama Vincenza was not one to murmur prayers in order to get her children to say them while she herself was busy about who-knows-what occupations. Rather, she watched with love to see to it that the children said their prayers well. When they grew older, she accustomed them to saying the rosary before they fell asleep. Whenever she saw that one of them had left the beads hanging on the bedpost, she would place them in the child's hands and say, "Pray more, pray more."

Mama Vincenza never studied asceticism, but a reflection such as this one, for example, is undoubtedly profound asceticism: "It's a bad sign when someone doesn't like to pray.... The young person who doesn't pray will certainly turn out bad."

When the boys had to get up for Mass on Sunday mornings, she would help them overcome their sleepiness and laziness with another of her reflections: "We need to attract God's blessings through sacrifice. Our guardian angel takes everything into account.... Then, if one doesn't get used to making sacrifices when he is young...." And she would leave the conclusion to them.

When it was a question of going to Mass, no obstacles were too great, even if there was pressing work to be done. "Then you can work faster and what you do will turn out better. Go! Hurry!"

The children had to pass in review: shoes, clothes, necktie, everything had to be in order, not only for Sunday Mass—but also for confession on Saturday evening. Since they had time, while they were on the way Mama Vincenza would suggest points to her children for their examination of conscience. Then, when they arrived at church her final recommendation would be: "Remember to tell the priest everything!"

Mama Vincenza was her children's first catechist, so it is easy to see why Teresa later became such a good catechist herself. The mother used visual aids also; in her simplicity she was thus very up-to-date. For example, she would gather her children in front of a picture that represented the presence of God. Then she would say: "You see, God sees everything, hears everything and takes note of everything. He will reward the good and punish the evil."

Friendships? Certainly her children were permitted to have friends and also to play games—but at the proper times, under her supervision and only with children she herself knew personally.

Once at Castagnito, during the celebration of carnival, the vice-curate passed by the Merlo house and asked Mama Vincenza if he could bring the children to see the celebration. Her response was such a flat and resolute "no," that the good priest remained speechless. As soon as she realized how abrupt she had been, Mama Vincenza made reparation immediately, although still holding to her refusal. She told him. "I'm happy that you thought of my children, but I know that today in the square there are many people blaspheming and speaking evilly. You can't plug up the ears of these children. It's better for them to stay at home; in any case, they can entertain themselves even here."

Mama Vincenza was a great educator of her children. She did more by conviction and persuasion than by punishment. Her children could never remember her scolding them while she was under the impulse of anger. For this reason she was effective.

Mama Vincenza died on January 18, 1947. Teresa was the one who most resembled her, not only in her physical features, but in her self-discipline and in her ability to command. "They told me that sometimes I am too strict," she said one day when the full responsibility of the Daughters of St. Paul had fallen on her shoulders, "but I inherited this character from my mother."

Naturally, such an upbringing was possible only because Teresa's father Hector was very much like Mama Vincenza. He, too, first did and then spoke. At Sunday afternoon Vespers, the children always saw their good father near the priest or in the choir, singing and taking an active part in all the religious functions. What is more, he kept his children near him. He saw to it that they arrived in church on time with their books in their hands, all ready to sing. If one of them had been late because he stayed to "finish the game," once they were home again, Papa Merlo would admonish: "It's not right to come to church late. The game can be finished after Vespers."

The children could easily accept a reproof of this kind not out of fear but because their father himself gave the example. At the first sound of the bell, he would drop even urgent work. And if he did it, they felt they could do it too.

Papa Merlo died on March 9, 1941, after he had had the joy of seeing several of his grandchildren growing up—the children of his oldest son, John, and his youngest son, Charles. As long as he could, he had followed the activities Maria Teresa was carrying out under the direction of Father Alberione.

A significant story is tied in with the pastoral work of his son, Costanzo Leone. When Costanzo became pastor of the parish in Barolo on September 22, 1929, a townsman, who certainly meant to compliment him, said casually to Mr. Merlo, "The people of Barolo are good. If your son is smart, everyone will love him and he can have an easy life."

"Easy!" replied the half-scandalized father. "I didn't let my son become a priest so he could take it easy. I wanted him to become a priest so he could work, and work hard! All the more so, now that he is a pastor. Never mind, rest!"

Just tell me, now, if this isn't a little compendium of priestly formation....

Here is one more story, regarding Teresa:

When she decided to accept Father Alberione's invitation and was preparing to follow him, the townspeople disapproved and tried to impede God's designs by critizing Father Alberione. They tried to advise Papa Merlo, who, instead, seemed decided to please his daughter. Since the opposition of the townspeople and neighbors continued, at one point he spoke his mind thus: "Listen, I can't understand why you are taking such an interest in this affair! Is Teresa my daughter, or isn't she? If she's my daughter, then let us decide whether we should send her or not. She wants to go. There's no reason why you have to be so concerned about it." Hence, Teresa owed her vocation even to her father to some extent.

The Sewing School at the Merlo House

Teresa's brother Costanzo tells us: "I don't know why, but I have amnesia regarding the time spent with my family when Teresa and I were little. I only remember that Teresa was very weak. Mama had to make special food for her—eggs fried in butter —and she made her take a tonic. Then I don't remember anything else. Oh, yes! She was away from home for a short period of time. She went to the Sisters of St. Anne in Alba to learn how to sew. That was after she had already finished her schooling. But I do remember her obedience and simplicity."

The picture of Teresa's early youth is nearly complete. All that can be added is the testimony of those her own age. They tell us she was very bright and quick, very diligent in school and always among the first in her class. It might look as though this image of Teresa was painted only to impress. Nonetheless, it is in accord with reality. Teresa actually possessed all these qualities. Almost without effort on her part, her will was formed to be a perfect copy of her father's and mother's. This strong will guided her toward a maturity rarely found in young people. As a consequence of this wise upbringing, she showed that kind of psychological balance and self-control that prompts people to say: "Even though she is still quite young, she has a personality."

After her First Communion, made at the age of eight, she attended church very regularly.

Her friends who are still alive assure us that even in snow or rain she would go to church quite early in the morning. Five years after her First Communion, she was confirmed by Bishop Re of Alba. It was around this time that her diligence in grasping

Christian truths was noted; soon she became a catechist and began to teach other girls. Her pastor trusted her, because he always saw her in the first pew, looking very recollected; she was accompanied by her little cousin, Antonietta Flora.

She even taught catechism to her brothers. This task was entrusted to her by Mama Vincenza, who wanted her children to win first prize in religion class. Naturally, everyone benefited from Teresa's teaching.

Since Castagnito was a very small town, the elementary school did not go beyond the third grade. In order to attend fourth grade, Teresa had no other choice than to travel daily between her own village and the neighboring one of Guarene. But it was no joke for her, with her poor health, to go to Guarene every day. This could not go on. Her parents, who were ready to go through any expense and sacrifice for their children's health, decided that she would take fifth grade subjects privately.

"I believe that Teresa's deep spirit of prayer," notes Father Costanzo Merlo, "was greatly influenced by her teacher, Miss Chiarla, who gave her private lessons." Miss Maria Chiarla immediately realized that her pupil was eager for knowledge and soaked in every word. Teresa asked questions continually.

In short, she would drain the teacher! Miss Chiarla was delighted and helped Teresa complete even her religious education, above all by giving her an example of her own balanced and deep Christian life. Teresa always remained very grateful to her teacher.

As was then common for all girls, Teresa decided to learn some type of work upon completing her elementary education. Actually, it was not

absolutely necessary for her to learn an occupation, but we can well understand how the example
of her parents and her own innate industriousness
could not allow her to think otherwise. And, in fact,
as her brother has already told us, she went to the
Sisters of St. Anne in Alba in order to learn sewing,
embroidering and lace-making. This was the skill
which—once acquired—was to permit her to give a
foundation to the initial work of Father Alberione.

Even in the sewing school she had a way
all her own of not standing out. (After all, even
physically, she seemed "reduced to the lowest
terms" and her mother told her jokingly more than
once, "You are so small that when you are in the
courtyard I can't tell you from the chickens.") She
spoke only at the opportune moment and would
bring peace when some discussion became heated.
This was always true. This reserved bearing gave her
a sort of distinction that inspired respect and admiration.

Her parents spared themselves nothing so
that Teresa could perfect her human and Christian
gifts. "A woman who doesn't know how to sew lacks
something," Teresa once heard Mama Vincenza
say. So Teresa went to Turin, where she stayed with
some family acquaintances, to perfect her sewing
skills.

She perfected herself so well that today we
would call her specialized.

In those times, anyone who knew her work
as well as Teresa did was like a mother hen who
attracts chicks. Thus, Teresa returned to Castagnito
only to find herself immediately surrounded by many
girls who wished to learn her skills, because they

had to prepare their wedding trousseaus, since at that time it was deemed an honor for one to embroider it herself. Under the gaze of Mama Vincenza, Teresa transformed a part of the Merlo house into a sewing school. Mama Merlo was proud of her daughter, who certainly had never been lightheaded, nor was she now, as she took up her new responsibilities.

The Ineligible Sister

Teresa Merlo's sewing school was a little different from others. Even if it wasn't written down in black and white, the daily routine was quite regular: work, prayer and spiritual reading.

Immediately Teresa had realized that these girls needed to learn not only sewing and embroidering, but religion as well. Families of that time did what they could, but not everyone learned parish catechism as well as Teresa did. So between her helpful hints on the correct manner of holding the needle, of cutting, of embroidering and all the other little secrets of her art, Teresa found the time and the way to attract the love and confidence of the girls, and then she urged them to pray.

Hence, during the day when she would ask them if they would like to say the rosary together, they were all of one accord. They were also happy to listen to a brief spiritual reading, commented on by Teresa herself.

A friend recalls the time she spent in Teresa's sewing school: "My mother sent me to learn to sew and embroider. I went to Teresa's house every day for about three months and still have wonderful memories of the time I spent there. She always gave me good advice and scolded me only when I was gossiping."

This same friend also recalls the times she accompanied Teresa when she went to teach catechism to the children: "On the way it sometimes happened that she would stop to console people who were torn by some sorrow. She would console them with good words, words that gave them courage and faith."

The same companion admits that one time she was gazing at herself in a little mirror attached to the back of her sewing box. As was normal for a girl of her age, she was admiring her good looks. Without a sound Teresa went next to her and gently closed the lid. "I didn't say a word. But I didn't feel bad about it either. I knew the lesson was a good one for me, because I was vain."

From such a life-style and in view of Teresa's actions, it was not hard to deduce what her aspirations were. Obviously, she did not intend to marry, but not because she despised the married state — which, in fact, she saw in a very good light because of her parents' example. But the experiences of her youth, her contacts with many girls her own age, who in general were not prepared to live an authentic Christian life; her contacts in catechism class with children who showed great ignorance of religious truths; her awareness of so many moral and material miseries that could not escape her gaze: all these factors had convinced her — some time ago already — that she should set out on a road of generous donation to the service of God.

As for how she could do this — in her own parish there were the Sisters of Cottolengo of Turin, and she had also come to know the Salesian Sisters of St. John Bosco while she was staying in Turin perfecting her sewing skills.

At the time of our story, any young girl living in or around Alba who desired to become a sister would simply consider entering the Sisters of Cottolengo or those of St. John Bosco rather than look beyond her own geographical region.

St. Benedict Cottolengo and St. John Bosco, together with St. Joseph Cafasso, Allamanno, Venerable Murialdo, and Venerable Francis Faà of Bruno, were all very famous and recent sons of the Italian Piedmont. The first two, especially, had planted flowering religious congregations in the garden of the Church.

Teresa decided on the Sisters of Cottolengo. Surely those in Castagnito lost no time in explaining their spirituality to the young woman, for they saw that she could assimilate it very well. Thus, she went to Turin, but after the required medical examination it was found that she was not suitable for life in the community because of poor health — anemia. In a word, they did not accept her and even advised Mama Vincenza to give her tonics and special foods. After this had been done, her condition was thought to have improved, and she returned to Turin for a checkup. The second result was worse than the first. This time the sisters pronounced Teresa ineligible once and for all, because she did not have sufficient health.

Father Pistone, the pastor of Castagnito, was the first one to rejoice over the refusal. If Teresa had left to become a sister, it would have meant a great loss to him. Who would have taught catechism? To him and to many others, Teresa was the most able catechist. When he saw her again he tried to appear sorry over the turn of events, but his heart was beating for joy.

However, Father Pistone had counted his chickens before they were hatched.

On the morning of June 27, 1915, Teresa gave Father James Alberione her unconditional "yes." She consented to begin living a life of consecration that was to follow a completely new road.

A NEW MISSION
FOR THE NEW CENTURY

An Unusual Typography

We have already mentioned the "night between the centuries," the social conditions of the times, the invasion of an irreligious and anticlerical press that by now influenced many strata of society, and the idea that Father Alberione had been turning over in his mind for a long time — the idea of forming an organization to carry out a new mission linked to an apostolate of the press. He spoke of this to his closest friends and asked their prayers for it.

Sometimes he would confide: "These journalists do not have a complete religious education. That is why their writings contain grave inaccuracies, whether in doctrine or in moral teaching. If they were to be censured, it would be difficult for them to have the humility to submit; thus, grave scandals would result and the danger of factions would be renewed. It is necessary to found a new religious institute which will have the apostolate of the press as its real mission."

His confidants objected that there were already many modern religious institutes that could shoulder this undertaking.

"No, no," the young priest would reply. "A new institute is needed, having as its chief purpose the apostolate of the press."

36

His idea began to take visible form on July 24, 1914, when the first typographical machinery and house furniture were moved into a building in the Piazza Cherasca, Alba. This was the beginning of the "Little Worker Typographical School," the germ of the future Society of St. Paul.

The first group, consisting of two boys, Desiderio Costa and Torquato Armani, had already grown to six by the end of 1914. They would be nine in 1915, fourteen in 1916, eighteen in 1917, eighty in 1921. This crescendo continues—one may say— even now.

The typographical school was inaugurated on August 20. World War I had just broken out, and it could already be foreseen that Italy would soon be involved, as, in fact, happened.

If one were looking at matters from a human viewpoint, a worse time for launching this new endeavor could not have been chosen. But beyond a doubt those poor instruments had the special help of God in laying the spiritual and human foundations of a mission that would extend itself throughout the world.

Later, Father Alberione said, "Certainly it took a great deal of faith—as I have written else-where—to try to even imagine that from that poverty-stricken house in Piazza Cherasca, a worldwide organization for the apostolate of the press would spring up. The first two boys in Piazza Cherasca were confronted by an old printing press, another smaller press and a few cases of metal type. In addition to setting type and printing, they had to fold and sew. Since they did not know the trade, they had to follow the direction of outside workers who came in to teach them."

Father Paul Marcellino, now stationed in Korea, tells us about those early days: "For us, faith did not consist only in believing the general teachings of the Church, but even more, in believing in the extraordinary reality and importance of our particular vocation, as it was presented to us in God's name by Father James Alberione, who appeared to us to be God's most qualified representative. Therefore, we considered every word that came from his mouth as having come from the mouth of God Himself. This was at a time when one could say nothing was visible and there was general doubt regarding Father Alberione and his dream of the apostolate."

In fact, it seemed to most people that Father Alberione was looking for the moon in a well. Few believed in his endeavor, and pessimistic comments were pouring in from all sides:

"You'll go bankrupt for sure."

"You'll be wasting your best years."

To this criticism should be added the conditions brought on by the war, inflation and many other things, jealousy and opposition, as can easily be imagined.

Still, the little group continued along its way. The boys tried to learn the techniques of printing and, when they were able, to study also. Naturally, in this setup one studied as best one could. With all the responsibilities the bishop had placed on his shoulders, Father Alberione had little time left to teach the boys. He was spiritual director of the seminary and director of the diocesan newspaper, *La Gazzetta d'Alba*. In addition, he carried out all his other priestly duties. And Father Alberione had not become a priest for the sake of the stipends!

A New Road for the Woman

The brief meetings that he had with his boys, especially in the evenings, proved to be very enriching and effective. They enthused everyone — Founder and disciples alike — with the ideal of the press. The Theologian explained that to the way of life that they were trying out could be united the religious life, the priesthood and the press apostolate. As soon as this ideal was uttered, it captivated those boys, who paid no heed to sacrifice and separation from family as they worked to make it a reality. Some lived to see the tree of the new Society of St. Paul grow; others, like Maggiorino Vigolungo, died in full activity, while looking to the future, full of faith, and generously dedicating themselves to establishing the foundation of this new family in the Church.

As regards the typography school, the boys learned so fast and so well that three years after its opening Father Alberione saw that he could dismiss the outside workers. The little sapling had already sent down strong roots.

While the boys were completing their apprenticeship, Father Alberione was starting another foundation. He had never been able to understand why women had been so long separated from the Christian apostolate. The most striking figures of womanhood generously consecrated to God — like Clare of Assisi and Catherine of Siena, to give only two examples — were so surrounded by light in the niches of their high spiritual perfection, that it took one's breath away just to look at them. And, especially, it left women themselves breathless (and not only the women of those times). Women had contented themselves with being good mothers, good wives, and, at the most, good religious, but in every case they had remained sheltered from the world, either within the four walls of the home or within the four walls of the convent.

That extraordinary soul, St. Vincent de Paul, had done something new in asking women to help him in his mission. He had sent them out — out into the prisons and hospitals — to heal moral and material wounds in a way which people of his times regarded as foolish.

Father Alberione saw the good that these and other sisters did. He knew by direct experience as a priest and guide of souls how meritorious and useful that feminine consecration was, in view of the widespread dechristianization; but he also knew that all this was now too little for the needs of the times. Something was demanded that would put woman in a position of collaboration in the modern field of diffusion of thought and information. Whenever he envisioned the apostles of the press, he did not think of men only; women, too, would be able to carry out the same mission.

In this regard he even wrote a book that has been reprinted several times: *Woman: Her Influence and Zeal,* in which he describes the woman associated with the apostolic mission of the priest. Because Father Alberione always thought of this apostolic activity in terms of the press, it took little to realize that he meant "the woman associated with the apostolate of the press."

From the idea to its realization the step was short, without doubt shorter than envisioned — not only because Father Alberione was a man who strongly wanted those things which he believed right, but also because a group of young women interiorly felt (otherwise, it would not be possible to explain this beginning) the desire for a new and modern

consecration. Father Alberione was moving ahead
as if groping his way, or better he was like a man holding many pieces of mosaic to be put together, seeking
to discover the best possible design they could make.

In order to start, since he wanted to start right
away, he had contacted Miss Angelina Boffi, a very
devout young woman, in order to ask her if she would
take these girls into her home.

But Miss Boffi had not understood what
Father Alberione intended to do. In fact, she later
confided that when Canon Chiesa (a holy priest of
Alba who helped during the first years of the foundations) and the Theologian had made the initial
request of gathering the young women in her house,
she had believed that they were speaking of giving
hospitality to young women who would be working
or studying in the city and would need a safe place
to stay. At any rate, this first group gathered in
June, 1915. They set up a sewing shop right in the
Piazza Cherasca where the typography for young
boys was located. This group of boys continued to
work there while living in Moncarretto.

Italy had just entered World War I. As was
already pointed out, a worse time could not have
been chosen. But that was how Father Alberione
was. Moreover, the little group of young women
immediately found enough to do, sewing shirts and
uniforms for the soldiers at the front. And it is well
understood that all this was an accidental beginning,
only in order to gather the girls together to await
the right time.

Because she worked for a company in Alba,
Miss Boffi did not have much time to watch over
these beginners. This was why Father Alberione
had looked for someone who could dedicate herself to this task fully. It was obvious that he viewed

as a sign of divine Providence the spiritual maturity of Teresa coupled with the specialization she had acquired precisely in the occupation of seamstress.

We can now pick up at the point where we left Teresa speaking with Father Alberione. In order to "see for herself" as had been decided with the Theologian and her mother, Teresa went to work in Piazza Cherasca, and, docile as ever, was completely submissive to Miss Boffi.

Buttonholes, Buttons and Printed Sheets

From this submission, one can already measure Teresa's spiritual stature. Anyone else in her place —with the degree of specialization and experience she had acquired in directing the sewing school at her own house—perhaps would not so readily have accepted the idea of being dependent. But when she had said "yes" to Father Alberione, she had not laid down conditions. Nor did she lay them down to Miss Boffi. She did not desire a particular task for herself. She placed herself in the row of those who were sewing shirts, making buttonholes and sewing on buttons, just as if she were learning for the first time. The work was always the same, monotonous and even nerve-racking.

The Theologian visited the sewing shop often and spoke with everyone, but in a particular way he conversed with Teresa, on his usual topic of the apostolate of the press.

Indeed, when the young women were occupying the same building as the boys, the latter had left a pile of printed sheets in a corner of the sewing shop. These sheets were part of the book I referred to earlier. "Look at this," said Father Alberione. "This is a book I wrote especially for you."

Then an incident took place which Teresa laughingly recalled even after many years. She thought of asking Father Alberione if they could use that book for spiritual reading at lunch time (because they also used to have reading during meals).

"It's too heavy," said Father Alberione.

"That's all right," replied Teresa, believing he was referring to physical weight, "if it's too heavy, we can rest it on the table."

Regarding this first period of the "shirt factory," Teresa herself has written something: "They were beautiful—those days spent amid piles of shirts and the rumble of machines. We occupied an area left free by the boys of the typography school. This made us often exclaim, 'Who knows when we, too, will be able to do the same work!' But we didn't dare add anything else."

We can see clearly from this that Father Alberione had already indicated to the young women that he wished them also to begin working at presses. However, he did not appear to be in any particular hurry. He wanted the little group to form a strong community before doing anything else. One day he said to them: "The most fortunate young women to whom God has given the singular grace of forming the first nucleus of the Congregation, must above all seek to be hidden, to root out any ambition, to cultivate a deep spirit of humility, of sacrifice, to seal their hearts with the most pure love of Jesus—in a word, to be His immaculate and generous spouses."

At the end of 1916, the "Women's Sewing Shop," as it was called, was transferred from Piazza Cherasca to Via Accademia. Here, the girls began to

offer a few religious articles, also. Now they were
able to do something besides make shirts. And, at
a certain point, books, too, made their appearance.
Finally, a small book center came into being. As the
latest "arrival," it was soon called "the New Book
Center." The name in itself was a program.

This was the seed of future book centers,
of the Daughters of St. Paul which are centers of
diffusion throughout the world.

Well-intentioned Criticism

For some time—since the war was entering
its final stages—the young women of Via Accademia
had no longer been sewing shirts and military uniforms; rather, they were helping in the work of the
typography.

They used their needles equally well to sew
together the folded sheets of the *Christian Doctrine*
booklets that the boys had printed. It was a very
reasonable setup: one group printed, and the other
group sewed. And, thus, the piles of books grew.
But we know how things go in this world, especially
when the so-called "well-intentioned" judge them.

As we have already said, Father Alberione's
experiment had caused a number of people to open
their eyes. These people were bothered by the new,
simply because it disturbed their laziness and obliged
them to make comparisons and bring their own commitment forth from the idleness in which they had
resolved to let it vegetate.

It was logical that such persons should find
reasons to support their opposition. For example,
one excuse was the collaboration between the young
men and women for the press (even though they

worked in separate quarters). Then: What did the
Theologian have in his head, to make women become
typographers? Since when did women leave their
houses to do such work? If they were going to become catechists, it would be different. That would
be a real apostolate, but what kind of apostolate could
this be, dabbing ink and glue around? It was utterly
ridiculous! No, it could not go ahead this way.

When people formulated ideas of this sort, one
can imagine how serene the work of those first
pioneers must have been! We talk of the external
environment, because within their own surroundings
those young men and women were happy and had a
faith that shattered the arrows which the most hardened opponents and scoffers let fly.

Nonetheless, there were those who felt more
highly invested with a certain social respectability
and whose words—or so they believed—had greater
influence. These people did not limit themselves to
mere criticism, but also denounced the new undertaking to the bishop himself. Needless to say, they
used well-phrased arguments aimed at showing His
Excellency the need to stop this affair which, when
all was said and done, would never give splendor to
the diocese of Alba. His Excellency should look at the
novel situation carefully, because if this train were
later to be derailed, what could be done? It would
be better to prevent trouble, these wise people suggested, than to intervene when things had gone too
far and in a direction that did not seem good.

Unfortunately, the criticism and denunciations
did accomplish something, and there was more than
one moment in which the new mission ran the risk
of being suppressed right at birth. Another reason for
this was that someone, who evidently knew something about canon law and thought it should be ap-

plied in this case, took the bother of calling the attention of Rome, no less, to this matter of the typography school.

These were dark days for Father Alberione. Fortunately, Bishop Re was a very balanced and profound man, as well as a man of real pastoral charity.

This Shepherd governed the diocese of Alba at a time when both modernism and anti-clericalism were putting the faith of many people, including some priests, in crisis. Bishop Re and another holy priest, Canon Francesco Chiesa, a professor of the diocesan seminary, knew how to distinguish between the errors propagated by modernism and the just demands for a renewal in ecclesiastical life, pastoral theology and presentation of the Christian truths. In short, their balance showed itself in connection with the need to understand and make distinctions at a time when people were applying the label "modernist" even to those who expressed legitimate demands or opinions that had nothing to do with the modernist error.

Bishop Re knew Father Alberione very well, and he trusted him so much that he had appointed him spiritual director of the seminary and director of the *Gazzetta d'Alba*. Imagine, then, whether he would give ear to the critics! He examined the various denunciations that came during that time only to become more aware of the strange superficiality of certain human reasoning, and certainly not to draw conclusions from them. Knowing the Founder of the criticized mission personally, he saw no need to gather information by underhanded means. When he learned, however, that the critics had turned to Rome also, he acted energetically, for Bishop Re knew how to be energetic when the need arose. Since even in Rome he was highly esteemed as a wise and balanced person, the tempest raging around the newly-founded Congregation began to die down.

But the storm was not over, because when the zealous opponents saw that the bishop and the Pope had turned a deaf ear to their appeals, they sought the assistance of the mayor, the undersecretary of the city and the prefect of the region. They presented the problem as if it had political aspects, and was — if not truly an affair of state — certainly one of those "activities" to be followed with a watchful eye. To translate from bureaucratic terminology, this meant: let us get rid of them, fast!

Hence, we can understand why, on the morning of December 8, 1917, when celebrating the feast of the Immaculate Conception, Father Alberione gathered all the boys and young women for a sermon that was rather forceful. He ended with these words: "I know that before coming to this house each of you heard criticism against it. Many of you had to fight real and serious opposition. Such trials are necessary to keep us humble and to remind us that God is the only One in charge."

That was the conclusion. But the beginning of the sermon was like the keystone of the new foundation. It was a discourse on fundamentals that would go down in the Congregation's history.

"We frequently speak of promoting the good press," he said. "Now, some people are already working for this, devoting a part of their time and energies to this end: some for honor, some for gain, some for enjoyment. We ourselves want to work neither for enjoyment, nor for honor, nor for gain. But by means of the good press, we seek the glory of God and the reign of Jesus Christ in society."

It was a decisive and clear-cut program. "This is an historic day," he added, "and must be recorded as such, so that those who come after us will know the humble beginnings of the Congregation. This, not for our glory, but that they may see how God makes use of His most wretched servants to carry out His great works."

It was an unforgettable day, and all those still alive recall it very well. For Teresa it confirmed her vocation and her new responsibility.

From Sewing Machines to Printing Machines

The young women alternated the sewing of books with the teaching of catechism and with study.

Canon Francesco Chiesa was somewhat of a protector to the newly-founded mission. As he followed the formation of the boys, so he took upon himself the duty of preparing the girls, even doctrinally. He was a highly-esteemed theologian and the author of many publications. As pastor of St. Damian's, where he ran a very effective religious education program, he called in Father Alberione's group of young women to teach catechism. The girls derived much from the lessons in catechetical methods that the holy priest used to give to all his catechists. Although this had not been planned, those lessons gradually proved very useful for the new mission the young women were beginning to undertake.

Teresa, who at that time was Miss Boffi's assistant, later recalled a memorable day during the summer of 1918, when she and her companions were called together for a conference.

This is how she recorded it:

"The Theologian said to us: 'Our Lord is offering you a beautiful opportunity to do good. It means taking over a diocesan newspaper — composing it, printing it and diffusing it — at Susa. Do you think you can do it?'

"There was a moment of silence....

"'What answer can I give His Excellency, Bishop Castelli, who asked for you?'

"'Father, you know how many we are and just how much we are capable of. Only Emilia knows how to compose — and very little. What can be done?'

"'You will come into the typography. You will learn. Our Lord, the Blessed Mother and St. Paul will help you.'

"'Yes, Father, we'll go.'

"'Then, should I accept?'

"'Yes, accept. We will go.'

"'Go with trust. You will spend some time in the background. Then God will make use of you.'"

Father Alberione said those last words with the most profound conviction. He was sure that this little sapling, the feminine branch of his Institute, would take root and grow up strong. Now, however, it had to be transplanted, removed from the warmth of its native environment, so that its roots would sink deeper and become stronger through the trials and difficulties that would not be lacking. Moreover, it had to mature in humility. In this, however, the young women would not have to exert much effort, for they could not have been any less suited for their task than they were.... As Father Alberione himself remarked, they were capable only of crying.

And, in fact, when they left for Susa on December sixteenth of that year, every single one of them cried. Father Alberione consoled them, assuring them that the boys would pray for them for an entire month. They had to succeed. They would succeed.

THE CRUCIBLE OF THE EARLY DAYS

That Night in 1918

Susa would be a crucible for that first group of young women, but if we look back two years, we see that Alba had also had its period of trial. Many details have been passed on by word of mouth that are not recorded in documented history.

Indeed, let us go back some steps further, to the period when Father Alberione was making his plans for the new Congregation and visited Benevello — where he met Maggiorino Vigolungo — and Narzole, the birthplace of Father Giaccardo, who in 1919 would become the first priest of the new Institute.

Perhaps it was really in Benevello that Father Alberione planned out many details concerning his foundation. He remained there for two months in 1914, as a guest of the pastor, Father Brovia, so that he could regain his health a little. The person who described the following episodes is herself a Daughter of St. Paul. She remembers two stories very well. One concerns Father Alberione's nightly confessions to Father Brovia, and the other his teaching of catechism classes.

In answer to the astonished expression of this young girl, who was amazed by the fact of those daily confessions, Father Brovia himself told her, "You know...sins of holy water."

While attending a catechism class taught by Father Alberione, the girl would become embarrassed because she could not remember her lesson, so she would try to hide behind a companion. "I was afraid my eyes would meet the penetrating glance of the Theologian, because I felt that he could read into the very depths of my soul," she said.

This characteristic of Father Alberione's was experienced by more than one person, including the author of this book, who knew the Founder for some years before his death.

In March, 1917, when the narrator of these two stories, accompanied by her mother, came to Alba to enter the Congregation, she was welcomed by Father Alberione. After a brief talk with her, he called one of the boys and said, "Accompany her to Teresa."

Miss Boffi, as we know, worked for a business firm in Alba and was absent for a good part of the day. Hence, as we can see from the words of the Founder, the one in charge of receiving new girls into the Institute was Teresa.

At that time Teresa was teaching embroidery to some of the girls from the area; at the same time she would take care of the small book center that consisted of a few books arranged side by side on a shelf. Copies of the *Gazzetta d'Alba*, the *Quotidiano catolico* and the *Momento di Torino* were also displayed in the center.

Their residence was located at No. 2 Via Accademia. Two large rooms on the ground floor housed a printing machine, a paper cutter and several cases of metal type, all of which had been purchased from an old printing shop in Canale. The living quarters were on the second floor.

A few days after the arrival of the young girl from Benevello, other young girls of twelve and thirteen also entered. All of them, the new and the no longer new, worked at setting type, under the guidance of Torquato, one of the oldest boys, who would become one of the first Pauline priests — Father Titus Armani.

Certainly their training was not without a purpose. In fact, every week at Via Accademia they set the type for some of the articles of the *Gazzetta d'Alba* or for parish bulletins. Once composed, these were taken to the School of Typography to be impaginated and printed.

That a "school" such as this had not been foreseen by those young girls and that it seemed truly new to them, is shown by the fact that almost all of them, one after the other, returned home. All of them, including the narrator of these stories, had thought that entering the Institute meant enrolling in a private school, from which they would emerge seven years later, carrying a teacher's diploma. Now, this was not really a private school, even though one studied.

The way in which they studied may be quickly stated: Since a good part of the day was spent in the typography, the girls could not attend public school. Therefore, Father Alberione taught classes every evening until, with great sacrifice, Miss Boffi finally prepared herself privately and, in 1918, obtained a teacher's license. It was during this period, in which another group of girls also entered, that the responsibility — let us call it that — of superior was entrusted to Teresa.

An incident that took place around that time deserves to be recounted. It was June, 1918, the eve of the Feast of Saints Peter and Paul. The house in

Via Accademia was astir with a curious kind of excitement. The first three young women, Angelina Boffi, Teresa Merlo and Clelia Calliano, were busy decorating a picture of St. Paul that hung in the first-floor room that served as a book center.

Up to this point, there was nothing strange. What impressed the narrator was an incident that took place the following morning. While she and another companion were still in bed, something wakened her, and without letting herself be noticed she peered out from under the covers just in time to see Teresa, who slept in the same room, leaving in her Sunday best. She also heard Miss Boffi and Clelia, who were waiting for Teresa outside the door, and then all three of them went downstairs very softly. A little while later she heard the familiar footsteps of the Theologian on the paving stones outside, the opening and closing of the outside door, and then complete silence.

At the customary hour for rising, the three were with the others again, preparing themselves as usual to go to Mass at the Church of St. Damian. However, at breakfast and throughout the whole day, one could clearly see an unusual joy on the faces of the three "nightwalkers." In fact, every now and then they would sing a little song, that was meaningful only to them. The last words were: "Up, sisters! Let us make a promise. This is the pact which makes us one!"

To make a long story short, the others, the "excluded," could easily tell that something had happened, and they expected to be in on the secret. But the three never thought of telling them. Hence, without wanting to, they made the others feel a bit jealous. Only after a few years did the group finally come to know that on June 29, 1918, the first three young women had privately professed their religious vows.

The Theologian—Temporarily Unfit

The fact that a war was going on left its own particular mark on the activity of the newborn Institute. During the summer of 1918, there were about fifteen boys. Their day was divided between work and study. As much as those first times permitted, they studied as they could, precisely because there was much practical work to be done.

Referring to those times, one of the first boys, now a priest, said humorously: "The solemn idea suggested by the word 'Founder' is completely incongruous with the picture of a frail little priest (Father Alberione) stirring a pot of corn meal mush, or tasting soup to see whether it was salty or not, while explaining the rules of logical syllogisms to a scanty group of boys, who were hungrier for the corn meal mush than for the philosophy. But there is absolutely nothing unreal about this sketch," he concluded, "and it expresses the life of those years very well."

It is not difficult for us to agree.

The fact is that the Theologian was called from all sides, and one cannot really know how he could be present everywhere at once. It was good that at a certain point he received help in teaching the boys from Father Joseph Giaccardo. Thus, Father Alberione could do without teaching syllogisms while cooking corn meal mush.

Among other things, it was wartime. The "little priest," whom the army had declared "unfit" once already—and this confirms the wonderful health he enjoyed—was called back for another physical.

It is easy to imagine what complications the absence of Father Alberione would have caused among that little group of boys and young women. They all set themselves to pray so that he would again be declared unfit so...they could make him "fit." They were not conscientious objectors nor did they consider the war an absurdity. They had just reasons of another nature. The boys and young women all reasoned alike: if the father of a family is missing, especially at the beginning—and Father Alberione had always told them that they were a family—the members become disoriented and no longer know how to go ahead, especially if they have little experience.

They all began to pray that the military doctors would find Father Alberione better suited for hospital service than for the front, no matter whether he had to console the wounded or absolve the dying. The young women even made a vow that if they received the grace they desired, they would give a large rug to the Church of St. Damian for the steps of the high altar. Because of the altar's size, this would certainly be no easy task.

On the day of the examination, one of the girls who was present in the book center relates that the front door opened, revealing the profile of a "young boy" dressed in a grey jacket and knickers. There was an air of mystery about him; with that cap on his head—like the ones worn by the boys of the typography school—you couldn't even tell how old he was. At any rate, the unknown personage opened his mouth only to say: "Tell Teresa they didn't take me." And he left, closing the door behind him. It had been like an apparition.

"All the more so," confesses the eyewitness, "because I ran out at once to see who the person might have been, but he was already turning the corner of another street."

In the meantime Teresa arrived, and the girl told her what had happened. A thrill of joy ran through Teresa: "But didn't you recognize him?" she asked. "It was the Theologian!" Quickly they set to work on the rug for the church, sewing together small remnants of cloth left over from the work the young women had done for the soldiers during the first two years of war.

At this point—in November, 1918, when the armistice had already been signed—two important events took place. The first was the painful trial of the terrible Spanish influenza epidemic which took the lives of thousands of people throughout Italy, claiming more victims than the war. One of the first three young women, Clelia Calliano, who seemed the healthiest and most robust among them, was stricken by a severe form of the illness, and it took her life in a short time. This was a trial for those young women and even for the boys. Happiness, even in the midst of privations, was their "daily bread." That unexpected death rooted them more deeply in the mystery of existence and spurred them on to greater dedication in those things that really matter in life and last forever.

The second event was the request from Bishop Castelli of Susa to print his weekly newspaper, *La Valsusa*. Its publication had been suspended during wartime, but now he wished to bring it back into circulation.

THE CRUCIBLE OF THE EARLY DAYS   57

For Father Alberione this offer was providential, since he had been waiting for an opportunity to introduce the feminine branch of his Institute to the techniques of printing. With this in mind, he had already made his decision to accept, but he had still wanted to hear the opinions of those concerned and have their consent. As we have already seen, the dialogue was somewhat embarrassing for the young women, but nonetheless they happily approved the project. There is no doubt that it was Teresa who prompted them to accept the proposal without hesitation.

The New "Preachers"

From that dialogue, it could be seen that "only Emilia knew how to compose." It was decided, therefore, that Miss Boffi would also learn to compose and to make layouts, while Teresa would learn how to operate the printing press at the typography school. In the meantime, two more girls entered, and the group began to take shape.

The preparations for the departure for Susa were made during the month of November. Miss Boffi and Marcellino, one of the most experienced boys from the school of typography, went on ahead to look over the situation and prepare for the arrival of the others. After a few days, on December 18, Teresa and the other young women also set out for Susa. They saw at once, however, that the typography provided for them by the bishop was inadequate for the work that they were expected to do. It was necessary, therefore, to find themselves another, with an adjoining book center.

Duties were assigned at once, according to the capabilities each had acquired. Together with the responsibility of the whole "platoon," Miss Boffi was given charge of the book center and the classes. Teresa was entrusted with the printing presses, while Emilia, with the aid of a boy from the printing school, worked on the composition and layout of the newspaper *La Valsusa* and shortly after, also of the bulletin *Nel Canto del Fuoco*. There were only two printing presses, and both models were antediluvian! It was often necessary to replace electricity by inserting a crank into an enormous wheel and running the press by cranking with all one's strength. This was tiring work and necessarily required shifts. Due to her poor health, Teresa especially felt the effects.

To the difficulties of the machines were added difficulties from the outside.

Since the war had ended only a short time before, things were not yet functioning as in normal times. Due to paper shortage, the newspaper and bulletin were frequently printed on poster paper of various colors. Moreover, since the "gears" of the editorial staff were not yet well lubricated, the writers delivered their articles very late. When this happened, it became necessary to continue working in the print shop far into the night. In spite of all this, the first issue of the new *La Valsusa* made its appearance in the first days of 1919, just two weeks after the arrival of Father Alberione's little group.

"You did a fine job," wrote Canon Chiesa to the young women, whose efforts he followed closely. "See how fortunate you are. In such a short time, you have mounted a pulpit to teach an entire diocese! What preacher in the diocese of Susa can boast of an audience as large as yours? You preach the Good Word to everyone.... But remember that the Word must be enlivened by the spirit, and put this spirit into every word you compose, every page, every copy of the paper that you fold or address." So much did this letter reflect the spirit of the new Institute, that it might very well have been signed by Father Alberione himself.

Teresa nourished herself on this spirit daily. She was grateful to Canon Chiesa, who always emphasized this spirit on any occasion that presented itself.

"You Will Do Even Greater Things"

Other girls from the vicinity of Susa entered the Institute; however, not all of them persevered, for certainly the whole life-style was rather strict. The manner of studying and working had nothing in common with that of traditional private schools. Therefore, either the newcomers would fall in love with the ideal for which the young women had come together, or they would abandon everything. There was no middle road.

The little communities—both that of the boys and that of the young women—were sustained and nourished daily by Father Alberione. He often traveled to Susa, too, and gave encouragement to the young women, who at that time were undergoing many difficulties.

However, to listen to those who were there at that time—what they remember most about that period is not the effort but the joy, the certainty of continual assistance from divine Providence, which guided all events with Its own hand. So many were the signs of supernatural help received in such various forms during those trying years, that one might say it did not demand a blind faith to believe in the love of God and in the mission Father Alberione had received.

It was there in Susa that Teresa really showed the nature of her interior life. Due to her poor health, she soon had to stop her work in the typography, but she was always the first to give a helping hand at any task. "With her simple, warm and spontaneous manner," her first companions recall, "she was the soul of everything: in housecleaning, in the kitchen, in the refectory, during recreation, in folding the printed sheets, and especially in lovingly assisting and guiding the younger girls. She did everything so well and so quickly that it was inspiring to watch her."

Her external activity in no way impaired her internal recollection. She always kept her motive in mind, that is, the reason for which she had decided to follow Father Alberione. Moreover, she never forgot the purpose of this new mission, which the Founder outlined more clearly with the passing of each day.

To Teresa Merlo, who had already perceived the idea of a vast expansion, it had already become evident that their numbers would have to increase in order to achieve the ideals of Father Alberione.

One significant episode from those times is enough to prove this. Among the writers of *La Valsusa*, there was a lawyer, Louis Chiesa, from Turin, who came every week to bring his article, and many times did not hesitate to help the girls with the composition, layout, and proofreading. In fact, he would even improvise additional articles when necessary. The lawyer was already quite captivated by Teresa's personality, but one day he was taken by surprise when she directed a well-formulated question to him: "When are you going to convince your two good cousins, Margherita and Gina, to enter our Congregation?"

Thus Teresa anticipated what she would do until the last days of her life: find "laborers," always new laborers, for the vineyard of the press apostolate. Besides, Father Alberione did not make any mystery of what awaited them in the future: "I don't know whether the thought sometimes comes to you," he said, "to compare our House, so little, with the other great Orders of men and women, who for years, and even centuries, have been accomplishing immense good in the Church and in society. Well, I tell you, all this is little compared to what the Lord desires, expects and asks of you...."

The "Daughters of St. Paul"

A typography all their own was something they thought a real luxury. To have everything at their disposition, to be able to do everything right there — composition, printing, binding and diffusion — was the ideal situation. The young women could not have asked for anything better.

They had lost no time in throwing themselves into their work as typographers. Then too, the old house placed at their disposition by the bishop had been put in order quickly — empty as it was. This was another reason for dedicating more time to work, without forgetting, of course, the exercises of piety and prayer in common recommended by the Theologian.

The young women immediately attracted the attention of the people of Susa. It wasn't an everyday matter to see women working in a typography. It

really didn't seem that they were working for enjoyment or material gain, at least as far as could be
judged from their deportment. Indeed, the people
were impressed by their way of doing things, and not
knowing the little community's name, they went by
the picture of St. Paul the Apostle on the book center
wall and began to refer to the young women as the
"Daughters of St. Paul."

It must be said that as early as 1915, Father
Alberione had designated St. Paul as the patron of
his foundations. In fact, he had gone to Turin pur-
posely to buy a picture of the Apostle. St. Paul's
image was placed in the entrance way of the first
houses of both the boys and the young women. That
the people of Susa, after seeing the picture of St. Paul
in the small book center, should start to call those
young women "Daughters of St. Paul" in their
Piedmontese dialect, was truly an indication of how
much approval this title received. After all, that
name corresponded to an entire program, a specific
spirituality—precisely that of the Apostle of the Gentiles, who used each and every means to spread the
message of Jesus. "If St. Paul were alive today, he
would have been a journalist"—so declared that
great man, Emmanuel von Ketteler, Bishop of Mainz,
one of the most ardent propagators of the Christian
social message in the last century.

Father Alberione repeated those words more
than once to his boys and to the first young women.
Teresa, in particular, remembered them well.

The first "St. Paul Book Center" was established in Susa. It was larger and had more stock than
the "New Book Center" in Alba. Having this book
center was a precious experience. And it was also at
Susa that the young women began to study regularly
in order to prepare themselves for their new mission

in the fields of the press and diffusion, without, of course, neglecting the daily exercise of their apostolate.

The year 1919 was a year of trials—even exterior ones. It really seemed as though someone was infuriated over the young women of the typography. Certainly, the devil has "put his tail in the way," they told one another. Devil or not, it was a fact that on November 12, a fire ruined the poor house they lived in. It occurred during the middle of the night and in the cold of winter. This was no small incident. A short time later, a part of the typography ceiling fell in, and it was a real miracle that Enrichetta, one of the girls, had moved away from the cutting machine only a second before the blocks of cement fell on it.

The next year, 1920, on June 4 to be exact, there was a terrible catastrophe—an explosion at the military fort of Pampalù, near Susa. The whole city was thrown into a state of panic—windows shattered, furniture flying, and doors flung off their hinges. It was similar to an earthquake but worse. This new hailstorm also fell on the house of the Daughters of St. Paul, which had recently been repaired to some extent; needless to say, the damage was immense. The one good thing about it was that none of the young women were hurt.

It may have been in gratitude for their escape from danger, as also because of their love and veneration for the Apostle Paul, that the young women celebrated his feast, June 29, with particular solemnity that year—almost as if to give public recognition of the voice of the people, who wanted them to be called "Daughters of St. Paul." Father Alberione had not yet definitively chosen the name of his masculine Congregation. First it was called the "Little Worker

Society," then the "School of Typography," and finally, in 1921, it received the conclusive title— the "Pious Society of St. Paul."

A Daughter of St. Paul who entered in 1919 says of Susa: "Those were really the beginnings.... How many sacrifices during those first years! They were years poor in material means, but rich in faith— faith in God, faith in the beauty of our mission. I said 'years poor in material means.' We had, in fact, a very poor house. There was no heat, and the windows, doors and floors were falling apart. Moreover, in some parts there wasn't even a floor, but only a covering of cement and packed earth."

A story related by an outside witness confirms this. It was November 6, 1921, when the installation of the new bishop of Susa, the Most Reverend Umberto Rossi, took place. He was a young bishop for those times—only forty-two. Outside the cathedral he was surrounded by a crowd of men and women, including the young women of the typography— about a dozen.

It was Teresa who approached the new bishop with great simplicity and begged him to pay a visit to their house. The bishop promised he would go, and the following morning he did. He went with his secretary, who still recalls the sight that met their eyes. In all his life, the secretary had never seen a house as poor as that first little house occupied by the young women. "I remember," he states, "that it tore my heart to see such great poverty. At the same time, however, I felt much admiration, because of the true happiness shining on the faces of the two young women in charge—Teresa Merlo and Angelina Boffi."

The bishop, who was expert in the typographical arts—having been the director of the newspaper *Corriere di Casale Monferrato* — was also moved at the sight of the poverty and good will of those "novices" formed by Teresa and Angelina, and he promised them all his help and concern.

Father Alberione had always said: "The houses that prosper must begin from Bethlehem." Not even from Nazareth!

Notwithstanding all this, there was much joy, much love and union, and much enthusiasm for this new kind of apostolate. With Teresa — for they had more contact with her — all would make plans for the future: the foundation of houses; the opening of new book centers and typographies; the printing of many books in various languages, even for the mission lands.... In short, in their enthusiasm they would divide the world up among themselves in order to evangelize it with the press. And in the meantime each one prayed and offered her sacrifices for the mission field she had chosen.

THE FIRST GROUP AROUND
MOTHER THECLA

The First Vows

On October 19, 1919, Father Joseph Giaccardo was ordained to the priesthood. He was the first among eight young men who, in July of the same year, left the diocesan seminary of Alba to join Father Alberione's group. Since the members had grown in number (they were now about eighty), it was necessary to provide a house more adapted to their apostolate and study.

For example, in that year, it was decided to print the newspapers *Il Momento* of Turin and *Lo Stendardo* of Cuneo.

Father Alberione had the first part of the building constructed, and in the years following he took steps to expand it according to the needs. The typography was enlarged through the purchase *en bloc* of another, which had gone bankrupt.

The group of young men took deep root, and the priestly vocations that matured were a sign of the authenticity of the new Congregation.

On October 5, 1921, thirteen young men professed the vows of chastity, poverty, obedience and fidelity to the Roman Pontiff. This was the first official act of the "Pious Society of St. Paul"

at the house of Alba, which would have as its superior until 1936 the Founder himself—Father James
Alberione.

A few months later, on June 19, 1922, three
candidates who had received their training in the
new Institute were ordained. It was the first "domestic ordination," so to speak.

These facts and dates are recorded here because they are linked in the plans of the Founder
with the development of the masculine and feminine
branches of his foundation.

For this reason, too, it is well to know what took
place in Alba during the absence of Teresa. Domestic
duties at the School of Typography were being performed by Mrs. Rosa Raballo and her daughter
Angelina. By this time, however, there was a large
number of boys, and two women alone could no
longer do all that was required for such a sizeable
community. The need was such that Father Alberione
appealed to all the pastors with whom he enjoyed
more confidence, asking whether they knew any girls
with tendencies towards religious life who would be
interested in joining the new Pauline Family. Father
Alberione would welcome them, even overlooking
possible difficulties of health or of another nature.

One day, Angelina Raballo confided to Father
Alberione her desire to become a sister. Since she
well understood the setup at Alba, she knew that he
would have to find someone to take her place there.
The thought never passed through Angelina's mind
that this new enterprise of Father Alberione's could
offer all the characteristics of a life consecrated
to God. The religious life-style of that initial group
seemed far from the traditional religious life she was
acquainted with.

Since the community of women was now in
Susa, Angelina had had no possibility of personal
contact with them, so it was Father Alberione who
opened her eyes. If Angelina wanted to become a
nun, he was very happy, but she could satisfy her
desire even by entering the new community.

Everything was clear to Angelina now, and she
decided to enter the foundation of the Theologian.
In a short time several other girls followed her.
Rosa Raballo assigned the work of mending, washing
or cleaning to each of the girls; but when a sudden
illness carried her to heaven, the women turned to
her daughter Angelina, who bore the responsibility
of the community in Alba. The girls were housed in
the convent of the sisters, Oblates of St. Aloysius
Gonzaga, and this same group soon opened a new
book center on Via Vittorio Emanuele II in Alba.

"I Appoint Maestra Thecla for Twelve Years"

"We had a premonition," recalls one of the
earliest members, "that sooner or later we would
leave Susa. In 1922, at the time of the scholastic
tests, Miss Boffi, I and two others went to Mondovì
to take the examinations. On our return, instead of
going directly to Susa, we passed through Alba to
visit our families, whom we had not seen for two
years. It was at this time that we received the surprise
news that we would not be returning to Susa, because
the Theologian wanted to bring the Institute back to
Alba, so that he could give us a formation adapted to
our special vocation."

Father Alberione wanted to forge ahead, and in
order to forge ahead he could not work with the

young women from a distance. It was necessary for him to form the feminine branch of the Institute directly, just as he was doing with the masculine branch. He had gone to Susa frequently, but the young plant could not be rooted well by giving it only an occasional sprinkling. The formation had to be daily, calm and intense, especially because it was a matter of a completely new form of religious life, one outside the traditional design. In fact, rather than withdraw themselves from the world, these young women had to learn to go into the world and carry out in it their apostolate of proclaiming the Christian message by using those same means that the modern world has invented and employs for the most extravagant ends.

Father Alberione also wanted to confide to the small group of young women everything that impelled him, just as he had done with the young men. He wanted to implant well into these souls — whom he considered called to a most sublime vocation of contemplation and action — the charism so ardently impressed on his own spirit by God.

So it was that in the latter part of July, 1922, Teresa and the others were called from Susa. After Father Alberione had joined them to the group of Alba, he gave them a three-day retreat. It was a special course of spiritual exercises, at the closing of which nine of the older and more mature young women professed their religious vows. On that occasion each one took a new name with the title of "Maestra" (teacher) in honor of Jesus Master, the Teacher.

It is necessary to explain the significance of this title, which was so typical of the new spirituality.

To place all the means of modern social communication at the disposition of the Word of

God is at once the genius and the spirituality of the Pauline Family. This concept, cultivated by Father Alberione from the beginning of the century, has found depth and acceptance through recent acts of the Church's magisterium: the conciliar decree *Inter mirifica* (Decree on the Media of Social Communication) and the pastoral instruction *Communio et progressio* (Pastoral Instruction for the Decree on the Means of Social Communication).

Among the various titles that can be attributed to Jesus, Father Alberione has given prominence to that of the Divine Master. When He came to live among men, Jesus presented Himself as Teacher. And He was acknowledged to be such by His disciples: *Teacher, Rabbi.* He also proclaimed Himself to be such:

"You call me 'teacher' and 'Lord' and fittingly enough, for that is what I am."

"Only one is your teacher."

"Go and make disciples of all nations."

The apostles who had learned directly from Christ taught others. From the teacher come other teachers, and from the Word come those who multiply the word: a Word that endeavors to form mankind and restore it to the design God has always had for it. Jesus-Teacher is, consequently, the "form" or "mold" of all Christians, and the apostles, too, made themselves molds.

St. Paul tells us: "Imitate me as I imitate Christ."

St. Peter says about the apostles: "They willingly became patterns to the flock."

St. Leo the Great states: "In vain will we be called Christians, if we do not conform our lives to that of Christ, who declared Himself to be the

Way, so that the life of the Teacher might become the *form* for the disciple."

The word *maestra* means teacher — that is, form or model.

To come back to the gathering of the young women in Alba — Father Alberione spoke to the group and expressed himself in these exact words: "From today on, Maestra Thecla will be your superior general. I have appointed her for twelve years, and after that you yourselves will see to the matter."

Thecla was Teresa Merlo's new name. Thecla had been the first disciple of St. Paul. That day Mother Thecla officially became the first disciple of the new Congregation — the Daughters of St. Paul.

In its evangelical sense, "first" signifies "one who serves." And, in fact, docile and obedient to the charism of the Founder, her life will be "one" with that of the newborn Congregation. It will be intimately woven into the trials, joys, successes and difficulties of the new religious family.

At one time, Father Alberione had asked the other girls what they thought of Teresa. Their reply had been full of enthusiasm. "For my part," stated one, "being near her gives me the same feeling that I have when I read the life of a saint and feel that I want to try to imitate him." At this, Father Alberione simply smiled.

In March, 1923, Mother Thecla again journeyed to Susa, to put everything in order and bring the whole community back to Alba.

After the appointment of Mother Thecla, Miss Boffi, who had given the hospitality of her own home to Father Alberione's first group, withdrew from the Congregation — first to join the Franciscan Tertiaries of Susa, and later to enter a monastery in Marseilles. In all probability she must have felt that she did not have the necessary qualities for this new form of religious consecration, so different from the traditional. Through her efforts, prayer and personal offerings, however, Miss Boffi continued to contribute to the development of the new Pauline family. In 1926, stricken with a severe illness, she passed prematurely to her eternal reward.

A Novice—Too Young

We know something about the life of the young women, after Mother Thecla's appointment as superior, from the account of a "maestra" who entered the community of Susa in October, 1922, at the age of only...nine.

From the questionnaire for acceptance, which the candidate herself filled out, it was understood that she was nineteen. After all other necessary matters had been taken care of, the little girl's father brought her to the Daughters of St. Paul. When Mother Thecla saw the child she was puzzled.

It should have been enough for the good man to see the conditions in which the young women lived, the rather uninviting surroundings and the work to be done—for him to realize that all these held no promise of good for a child who needed much care. Mother Thecla made him understand that even though she felt regret she could not accept the little girl.

The father of our "maestra" then explained that his wife had died only a few months before, leaving him with this one little girl and her five brothers. There was no one who could take care of her. "If she stays at home," concluded the good man, "she

will become a girl of the street." This was enough
to deeply impress Mother Thecla, and at once she
decided to accept the girl.

Naturally, the child had to be completely
formed—even humanly speaking. What is more, in
those first years she suffered greatly from home-
sickness, so much so that at Christmas time she
wanted to go back to her family. However, Mother
Thecla succeeded in having the child make a promise
to return. She did, in fact, return, and Mother Thecla
herself prepared her for her First Communion, which
she had not yet made.

From this same source we have learned about
the beginnings after the transferral to Alba, which
took place in 1923. Mother Thecla mitigated the
punishments that had been enacted there for small
faults. For example, it had been customary to impose
a punishment for breaking the silence, carelessly
overturning an ink well or other such things. Pardon
for faults was to be asked at mealtime. After saying
grace, the "culprits" had to remain standing until the
spiritual reading was over, and then they would ask
forgiveness before the entire community.

Mother Thecla changed this practice immediately. Pardon was to be asked before the spiritual
reading, so that no one would have to eat cold soup....

Little by little, all of these small punishments
were eliminated. The younger members were taught
to act out of love for God. They were instructed to
live in His presence and perform all their actions
conscientiously and responsibly, trying their best not
to offend God and neighbor.

In a word, they were not to act out of fear, but
rather out of love. The psychology of Mother Thecla
nourished itself on the direct source of the Christian
message. For this reason she knew how to select and

guide the girls, winning the confidence and correspondence of all of them.

Mother Thecla had a truly unique mission: to
be *the* faithful interpreter of Father Alberione's
thought regarding the feminine Congregation of the
Pauline Family. In this Congregation she had to form
responsible members for a vast mission that would
spread throughout the entire world. From the moment she had said her "yes" to Father Alberione on
that day in 1915, Mother Thecla had felt all the
weight of this obligation.

It is easy to imagine how the new apostolate
encountered great difficulties from the very beginning, even because it was something altogether new,
especially for those young girls, the majority of
whom had come from country towns and were completely inexperienced.

While forming them both humanly and spir-
itually, Mother Thecla patiently introduced them to
the techniques of printing. She always sought ways
to facilitate work in the book-bindery and the field
of diffusion. Many episodes from those early years
are still recalled by the first young girls.

They were few, and since there was much to be
done, whether it was housework or the production
of books, they would continue to work into the wee
hours of the morning. Before Mother Thecla would
go to rest at night, she would go to see her "daughters," show her interest in their work, help them with
it and then recommend: "Tomorrow try to make up for
the hours of sleep you are losing tonight."

Mother Thecla had set out on the path of *total
giving*. When she saw that things were not moving
ahead well, she would not hesitate to attribute the
fault to herself. Even during breakfast she would

stand up and ask forgiveness of everyone for her bad examples, saying that she was the cause of the lack of grace in the community.

When the community had gathered to celebrate the Feast of St. Thecla on September 23, 1924, Mother Thecla knelt in the midst of the small community and said aloud: "I feel a need to ask forgiveness from each of you. If vocations do not enter, it is my fault, my sins." The mistress of the youngest members pleaded with her not to continue, and Mother Thecla stopped immediately. To promote new vocations was her fixed idea, because she saw how much the new mission needed them.

In that same year, one of intense activity, some of the boys from the Society of St. Paul brought into the apostolate room (the name at that time for the place where the technical apostolate was carried out) freshly printed sheets of the first edition of the Gospel. Father Alberione, who was present, took this occasion to sketch with a few bold strokes the apostolic perspective for Mother Thecla's small band of young women: "The production and diffusion of the Gospel is your specific mission. There will come a day, not far distant, when you will distribute thousands and millions of copies of the Gospel to people of every nation and tongue. God has prepared great things for those who are faithful."

(Some remember that on this same occasion, Father Alberione also predicted that "the train will come to the house and be filled with our publications"; this has now been realized through the most widely-circulated Pauline periodical—*Famiglia Cristiana*—which is shipped via a train that goes directly into the printing plant to be loaded.) To hear him speak, one might have thought that Father

Alberione was fanatic. No one could foresee, then, that the reality itself would be greater than the prophecy.

The entire group of Daughters of St. Paul drew near to those first printed sheets of the Gospel. It was truly a great event. Each one kissed them respectfully: fundamentally those sheets represented the purpose for which they had consecrated their lives. From that time on, the Gospel has always enjoyed special veneration in the Pauline Family and is displayed in every house.

A memorandum that was drawn up for legal use shows that during this era in the history of the Paulines the masculine and feminine branches numbered six hundred members. They had about fifteen printing presses and several type-setting machines. Approximately 3,300 pounds of paper were used daily in the printing of books, periodicals, 300 parish bulletins, catechisms, Gospels, lives of the saints, etc....

This was extensive work. In contact with the apostolic dynamism of Father Alberione, Mother Thecla refined her natural gift of industriousness and, above all, those supernatural gifts of humility and unshakeable faith.

After all, in the Founder's design, she was destined to represent the perfect example of the "woman associated to priestly zeal" which was the subject of the book we have already mentioned, written by Father Alberione and published some years before—a book that is read with much interest even in our own time. Many decades before the appearance of the encyclical *Pacem in terris*, the young priest of Alba had indicated the emancipation of the woman as a sign of the times.

"The woman of today," wrote Father Alberione, "must form the man of today. She must provide for his needs and serve him through the means available today." This was a profession of faith in the capability of the woman to contribute to the development and reformation of civil and ecclesial society.

"The woman of today," he continued, "must be better instructed in the Faith than the women of past centuries. She must have a greater degree of foresight into the objections and difficulties that the faith of her child will encounter in the world. She cannot throw him into the midst of ravening wolves like a defenseless lamb; she must arm him with an instruction that is more complete."

Having lamented that young people drift away from the Faith after they have reached the age of twelve or fourteen, Father Alberione affirmed that among the various causes, "not last is that of a mother who cannot give what she doesn't have — a more abundant religious instruction, a character that is stronger when faced with the thousand seductions of the world."

This ideal of the woman Father Alberione saw in Mother Thecla. But he also entrusted to her the task of giving rise to and actualizing the same ideal in all the young women who had followed her. The docile one-time seamstress of Castagnito d'Alba had embraced this tremendous duty with complete trust in divine Providence.

ROME CALLS

The First Sisters in the Capital

By this time, the young plant had begun to take firm root. The group in Alba could no longer fit in their small quarters. Moreover, Father Alberione's ideal — to proclaim the Gospel message through all the most modern and up-to-date means of social communication — was a universal one. And then, there was the call of St. Paul, after whom the new mission was named: a powerful call that came from the center of Christendom, where the great Apostle had sealed his witness to Christ with his own blood. Perhaps Alba was only the beginning. The new apostolate ought to take new impetus from the center of Christianity and launch out to every continent, fostering vocations among young people who would put themselves in step with the times and give their lives in total consecration for the diffusion of the Gospel message.

Father Alberione took the Holy Year of 1925 as a good occasion to send a priest to Rome with the task of finding a suitable location "to pitch the tent." And, it is logical that the Founder would suggest that the priest look for a site "near the Basilica of St. Paul." The young priest lost no time in finding a house at Via Ostiense 75/1, which was later described in the history of the first years as "a location not very ideal."

At the end of the Holy Year, Father Alberione went to Rome himself to see the location. Because he was accustomed to holy adventure, the Founder at once judged the location good enough to begin with.

On January 14 of the following year, the first group of young men, under the direction of Father Joseph Timothy Giaccardo, left Alba.

In a big hall near their residence, the Paulines began to publish the bulletin for parishes in central and southern Italy. This work had previously been done in Alba, but was now given to the group in Rome, because the area for distribution was closer. At about the same time, a new weekly newspaper was introduced—*La Voce di Roma*—published in four different editions for four different dioceses.

To give a more detailed account, it is well to know that in April of the same year, there were at least sixty-three bulletins printed in Rome. In addition were printed *L'Acaldo di Volterra*, *L'Unità Sabina* of Rieti and *La Voce del Popolo* of Monte-fiascone.

The Daughters of St. Paul certainly did not fall short in their own conquest of Rome. In fact, the same day the young men arrived, the first sisters, too, reached Rome. They settled in a small but dignified villa at Via del Porto Fluviale 7. They stayed there for a full year, until the landlord asked them to leave. Then they moved into what had previously been a warehouse for hardware near the residence of "Father Giaccardo's boys," as they were called in Rome.

The sisters also began to alternate with the boys in the typography. Often working overtime, they took one shift while the boys took another, so that the composition, printing, production and shipping of the bulletins and newspapers could move ahead at a rapid pace. (*Il Faro del Golfo* and *La Voce del Mezzogiorno* were soon added to the already-mentioned titles.)

In November, 1927, the Daughters of St. Paul purchased a piece of land from the Benedictines on Via Grottaperfetta — and settled down in a rustic farmhouse. Soon enough this proved to be inadequate in size; in fact, some of the sisters had to adapt themselves as best as they could to sleeping in a dilapidated old hayloft that was at the mercy of the rain, wind and every other kind of inclement weather.

They were truly adventurous times, but all who were involved remember the deep joy that united them and the generosity with which they dedicated themselves to the printing of the newspapers and to the apostolate, and to looking for new vocations.

At the Market with the Mule

Meanwhile, not only did the sisters in Alba pray for the first community that had "pitched camp" in the capital, but they also set themselves to work so that help and means would not be lacking. It even seemed — to use military terminology — that Alba, the area behind the front lines, was busier than Rome, the advance post. Surely Mother Thecla worked tirelessly.

After the joy of the diocesan approval of the masculine branch — under the name "Pious Society of St. Paul" — on March 12, 1927, the work of Father

Vincenza Rolando and Ettore (Hector) Merlo,
Teresa's staunch, devout parents,
whom the townspeople admired and respected.

Teresa Merlo's home in Castagnito d'Alba

Cradle of the infant Teresa

Bedroom of the youthful Teresa, revealing her fine and industrious nature.

**Teresa's first meeting with Father Alberione took place
in the Church of St. Damian.**

At the age of 21,
Teresa knew her
vocation in life.
With
Father Alberione,
she undertook the
great work of
founding a
Congregation for
women to be known
as the Daughters
of St. Paul.

First photograph in
the religious habit.

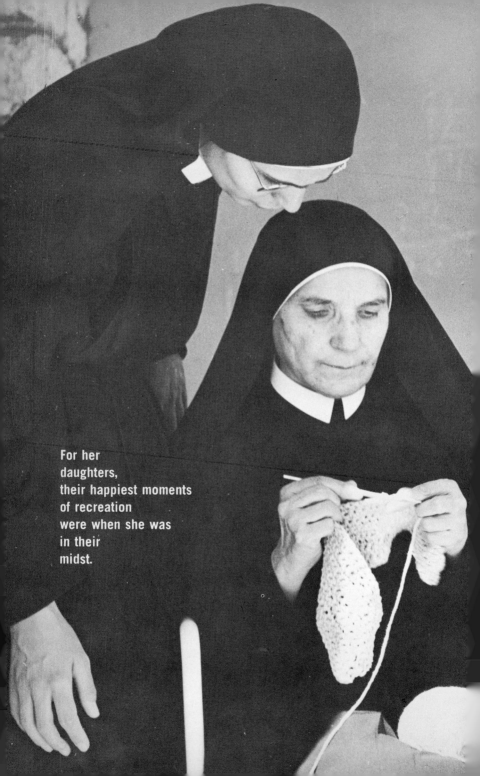

For her
daughters,
their happiest moments
of recreation
were when she was
in their
midst.

She was the ideal Pauline
and perfect model of observance of the Constitutions,
her favorite subject for conferences.

Mother Thecla
traveled around
the world
several times
visiting her
daughters
in over
twenty-five
nations...

Brazil

Philippines

Korea

India

Mother Thecla
with
His Eminence,
Paul Emile Cardinal Leg
who welcomed
the Daughters of
St. Paul to
Montreal, Canada.

Convent of the Daughters of St. Paul in London, England

Mother Thecla
with a
new-found
friend
in Japan.

Mexico—
Mother Thecla at the
ground-breaking ceremonies
for the new convent
in Mexico City.

Mother Thecla on the occasion of her visit to the
Daughters of St. Paul in the Congo

The community of Sydney, Australia

Formosa

Uganda

**Mother Thecla received a warm welcome
from airline officials on her last trip to the U.S.**

One of the
St. Paul Catholic Book and
Film Centers in the United States

The American Novitiate
of the Daughters of St. Paul
in Boston, Massachusetts

St. Thecla's Retreat House, Billerica, Massachusetts, named for Mother Thecla.

Alberione was more clearly understood, and, as he foresaw, the feminine branch would soon receive diocesan approval also.

Father Alberione often said that deeds are what count. Although he was very careful about giving precise form and juridical structure to his undertakings, according to ecclesiastical norms, he was above all interested in the content of his apostolic work. The more he saw apostolic needs grow, the more he felt the demand for new vocations, especially for the feminine branch. He frequently spoke about it to Mother Thecla, communicating to her his own apostolic zeal. She did not keep this only for herself, but in turn succeeded in communicating it to all the other sisters.

Many episodes could be cited regarding life during those years. They sound like the *Fioretti* of St. Francis.

One sister recalls that on a certain day in 1927, when a market was being held at St. Damian's, Mother Thecla arose early and said, "Let's go to the market with the mule!"

Mother Thecla adapted to everything, and since the sisters could not yet permit themselves to have a car, even a good mule could serve the purpose. During the trip, which was necessarily a little slow, Mother Thecla did not lose time; not only did she pray with the sister, but she also communicated what she felt within herself regarding the press apostolate.

Referring to the beginnings, she said, "The apostolate of the press is the apostolate we were to carry out in the future and spread throughout the world. But at that time we could see only the simple beginnings of it—or rather, nothing at all."

Another episode, dating from the first days of 1928, shows us the first community of Alba, numbering about eighty, gathered for night prayers. The sister who recounts this episode was eleven or twelve at the time.

She arrived in the evening, accompanied by her father, just at the conclusion of night prayers. Mother Thecla was giving a thought for reflection. "We have filled the second page of the new book of our life," she said. (It was January 2.) "What did we write it with? Gold? Ink? Water? And that is, did we conduct ourselves with charity? Or with superficiality and without the right intention?"

The young girl was deeply impressed and wrote later, "Mother Thecla seemed to be all spirit. She appeared transparent to me. So, you can imagine how happy I was the next morning to see her come into our little classroom to teach us arithmetic. There were about ten of us in the class, all either eleven or twelve years old. Before starting the lesson, she had one of us read a passage of the Gospel. I never forgot how recollected Mother Thecla looked as she listened to the word of God and with what gentleness and love she kissed the pages of the Gospel at the end of the reading."

The girl was also struck by the respectful attention with which Mother Thecla spoke to each pupil: "Her composure and bearing were so harmonious that I did not tire of watching her. But at the same time she inspired in me a sense of respectful veneration."

As was customary, work alternated with prayer. In May, 1928, the spiritual exercises for the youngest members lasted three days. During that time, they went to work in the bindery for an hour a day. "One day," the same girl continues, "I saw the superior,

Mother Thecla, suddenly appear beside me. I was only twelve years old, but swiftly, simply and politely, she helped me with my work."

She also describes what Mother Thecla would do when she came into the apostolate room. "She sat and wrote at a little table made out of a wooden case. Every so often she raised her eyes and looked at us with an expression that cannot be explained. It always made me feel better."

A Surprise—The New Habit!

Some nights during September, 1928, were different from the others. After the sisters had retired, Mother Thecla and a few other sisters would set to work, armed with scissors and black material. Surely, it had to do with a uniform. Indeed, since some sisters were neither deaf nor blind, they began to imagine that the Founder and Mother Thecla had decided something out of the ordinary. September passed, and then, towards the end of October, the mystery was unveiled.

It must be known that until that time Father Alberione had never told the sisters to wear a religious habit. He had believed that without it they would be freer and better able to mingle with people in order to carry out their apostolate. However, now it was no longer opportune to do things so simply. The Pauline family had grown and was becoming a sturdy tree with many responsibilities.

The Church had not imposed any habit. But, after reflecting, Father Alberione and Mother Thecla decided that the habit would be a tangible, external sign of consecration and even a type of protection for the Daughters of St. Paul.

In short, after supper on the evening of October 27, at about 8:00 PM, Mother Thecla called the sisters to her room. She gave each one a long, black dress, very simple in style, but nonetheless graceful, with a white collar and a jacket modeled on the style of the day. In addition, she gave each of them a small crucifix and a type of medal, or rather a little pin cut in the form of the Gospel, with an image of St. Paul on it, and with a cross, a pen and a lily in the background. To complete the outfit, all were given long veils of black silk. This was the habit especially designed by Mother Thecla for the first sisters. One of the sisters involved says of those days: "During October, 1928, we always worked at night, because the new habit was to be a surprise for the community. Mother Thecla was with us and directed the work, since she herself had designed the habit."

One morning Father Alberione, who wished to stress the importance of this event with the proper solemnity, wanted to bless each habit and give all the sisters a special conference suited to the occasion. Generally, Father Alberione never gave sermons "for occasions"; rather, he used every encounter with them to reinforce within them the ideal for which they had consecrated themselves to God.

The reception of the habit took place in the Church of St. Paul. It was the last Sunday of October, 1928, the Feast of Christ the King. The kingship of Jesus seemed to be a prediction and confirmation of the apostolic success of those young girls who tasted a special joy that day.

Distribution in the Families

That Sunday in October, 1928, saw not only the event of the religious investiture of the first

Daughters of St. Paul, but also the beginning of distribution in the homes. This type of distribution was also called "propaganda."

Today, the word *propaganda* means "publicity": to sell a product or to diffuse an idea and make it penetrate. Propaganda has become an art requiring an almost scientific preparation with its own terms of marketing, its own research and discoveries. After having taken advantage of newspaper pages, billboard posters, and films, people have recently become aware that contact with the consumer or the recipient of the message is always the more effective way of distributing a product. No other form of direct contact can match in effectiveness that of visiting homes. This form produces the most fruitful results, as commercial representatives and political candidates have always known.

Even at the time that the Daughters of St. Paul began distribution in the families, homes were already overrun by regular peddlars and salesmen. It came as a real surprise for many families to open their doors and find themselves face to face with two smiling young sisters who offered them, instead of dresses or beauty aids, books and magazines.

The Daughters of St. Paul thus became "bearers of the Word," directly contacting men and women to whom that Word—the Word of God—had been addressed for centuries.

Father Alberione's dream was becoming a reality.

Just as others offered their own products, so these young women began to climb the steps of every house and penetrate into every quarter of the city, every village in the countryside, to present books which offered the Christian message. Mother Thecla knew how to give her sisters opportune guidance for this work, which was certainly not without its difficulties. In fact, as we can imagine, not every door opened so easily; some, indeed, were slammed shut impetuously through religious indifference or scorn. But these were exceptions; as a rule, apostolic home visitations were exactly suited to the needs of the times. Mother Thecla decided to try this new form of apostolate herself, so as to have first-hand experience, which would be useful to pass on to her daughters.

It is interesting to know how this form of apostolate in the homes originated. By this time, the Pauline boys and girls were producing religious books, besides periodicals and leaflets. Diffusion, however, had not kept pace with the accelerated production. Father Alberione thought about this; in fact, he sought the advice of a collaborator. And since preparations were being made for the canonization of Don Bosco, it was thought that a biography of the saint, if written in a popular style, could easily be diffused in the families. And this was exactly what came about. Along with the life of Don Bosco, moreover, they were able to diffuse many other books and periodicals in the homes — for example, the holy Gospel and the lives of the saints.

It was like a little spark that immediately burst into a great blaze. Many towns in the diocese of Alba were visited in this form of diffusion.

The Daughters of St. Paul traveled two by two, a sister and an aspirant. "We would leave on Saturday," one of them recounts, "and generally we stayed out until Monday or Tuesday. We used a cart pulled by an old horse. This means of transportation ordinarily accommodated three teams of propagandists."

Mother Thecla went first with one team and then with another, to encourage them and to see the situation firsthand. Also one of the very first members of the masculine branch transported some of the teams of sisters in a little, old truck.

After the experience in Alba, two sisters were sent to Verona to experiment with the same form of apostolate there. The bishop of that diocese wanted every home to have a book or leaflet with his blessing and greetings. It was one way of carrying out this mission in that city.

The sisters of Rome, too, began to go two by two throughout the city and the surrounding area.

During the last part of that same year—in November, to be exact—other houses were opened in Salerno, Bari and Cagliari, as well as in Verona, as mentioned above. Then came the houses of Udine, Palermo and Reggio Emilia. Indeed, the three daughter houses of Verona, Bari and Salerno were really started by Mother Thecla, who chose to accompany the first sisters and stay with them for the first few weeks in order to start them in their work of diffusion through the book center and apostolic visits to the families.

Difficult Beginnings in the Book Centers

The opening of new houses came about in a rather unique fashion. The sisters—usually only two of them, for they set out in twos or at the most in fours—carried suitcases full of books. When they arrived at their destination, they would forward their new address and have more packages of books sent to them. Meanwhile, they would ask hospitality of the sisters of some religious community and, without losing any time, begin distribution in the families on the day after their arrival. As soon as funds permitted, they would rent a room—a simple room— where they made the best of things. Sometimes it wasn't even a regular room, but an attic.

Once they had taken care of their lodging—and certainly, I repeat, this lodging did not mean a well-furnished house, but simply a "hole" which kept the rain from falling on one's head and protected one from the wind and sun—after taking care of this, they at once made plans for the book center. Of course, a center could not open without some furniture. It was also necessary to go through all the civil formalities required for the opening of a bookstore.

I let you imagine what all this work of searching for a lodging, distributing books house to house and making arrangements at the city hall meant for these young sisters, who, all things considered, were only good girls, who had never seen any place beyond their native district and were certainly not accustomed to all this. However, the patience and constancy with which they succeeded in what they had to do and the kindness and charity that they exercised in all this activity yielded results that were often marvelous.

And even if someone complained about these strange, consecrated women who seemed to be more salesladies and business representatives, there were also others who understood the immense good they were accomplishing.

In order to give them strength, Father Alberione would tell them: "Don't worry—this is the will of God."

It was a good tonic in the midst of their sacrifices and disillusionments. Misunderstandings were never lacking, and there were people who believed they were giving glory to God by placing obstacles in the path of these young sisters.

For this reason, when the time came to open a new house, Mother Thecla would often make a last-minute decision to accompany the sisters. Upon their arrival she herself would help them find a place to live and a location for the book center, starting them out in the apostolate.

So much abnegation, in addition to the many benefits resulting from this new form of distribution, could not help but strengthen the ecclesiastical authorities' confidence in the young Congregation. Therefore, on March 15, 1929, the Congregation of the Daughters of St. Paul received diocesan approval, and the sisters made their public religious profession. Mother Thecla was officially named superior. The first draft of the constitutions — that is, of the rules of the new religious family — was printed for the occasion.

This ecclesiastical approval gave a new push to the apostolic expansion of the Daughters of St. Paul. In 1929, they also opened houses in Genoa, Messina, Catania, Foggia, Bologna, Naples and Catanzaro. Regarding Rome, one detail must be noted: in 1929, the sisters were permitted to diffuse their publications on a regular basis at the Basilica of St. Paul.

At last the ice had been broken, and news of the good done by these young women spread from diocese to diocese. The Daughters of St. Paul now went to places where they had never dreamed of going.

Trying to accept all the requests that came from all over was Mother Thecla's constant anxiety. For this purpose she continuously did her utmost to recruit, form and help vocations.

The Daughters of St. Paul carried out their new apostolate with such notable effects that even the Sacred Congregation for Religious asked an account from Father Alberione. Certainly, they did not have to ask him twice. In July, 1931, he wrote a very concise report: "In these years the Daughters of St. Paul have visited all the parishes in 246 dioceses [he enclosed the list]. A good number of bishops have encouraged them, insisting that they visit the parishes in their dioceses. The fruits of this apostolate have been many. We recall some: the moral-religious periodicals of the Pious Society of St. Paul now have 1,300,000 subscribers all together; approximately 3,000 parish libraries have been set up; in addition, 600 parish bulletins are being printed and diffused; over 1,000,000 copies of the Gospel, the Letters of St. Paul and the Life of Christ have been printed and diffused; 50,000 copies of the Family Bible have been printed, and four new editions are being printed right now. Every year, 600,000 copies of various lives of saints are diffused among the families. A number of bishops have requested the presence of the Daughters of St. Paul.... This little good, which we would like to see multiplied in accordance with present-day needs, is for the most part the fruit and merit of the fatiguing apostolate of the Daughters of St. Paul, who are invested with the same spirit as the Pious Society of St. Paul: spreading the doctrine of the Church by means of the press."

A report of this type is staggering. To have visited 246 dioceses meant that 80% of the Italian dioceses had been visited.

Astonishing also are the figures of the books and magazines produced by the Pious Society of

St. Paul. But acknowledgement of effective collaboration and the merit of this fatiguing apostolate are clearly and obviously given to the Daughters of St. Paul. Moreover, the sisters themselves were frequently able to realize — even firsthand — how much good many people derived from this form of diffusion.

A story is told of a press correspondent for a daily newspaper who returned to the sacraments after forty years, once he had read "Make Your Easter Duty," a leaflet that the sisters had left on a table in a large hotel.

Another story is told of the father of a family who went into a book center of the Daughters of St. Paul to relate the following: "I was about to commit some crimes. I wanted to kill my wife, my sick son and then myself, and I was just waiting for the right moment, with a revolver in my pocket. Then I heard a knock on the door and two sisters entered. The leaflet they left me insensibly drew me here to you. I really want you to help me to trust in God again."

A young woman, too, was grateful to the sisters because a biography she had laid on the bedstand of her father, a gravely-ill Mason, had persuaded him to receive the last sacraments.

These episodes tell us of the special graces employed by Providence in aiding the first steps of this courageous band, who did not spare themselves even when faced with the greatest sacrifices.

Some sisters have called to my attention "the great work of the Bible," carried out during 1931. In collaboration with the masculine branch, they were to produce numerous editions of the Sacred Book in a large format and in various languages (Italian, French, Spanish, Portuguese and English), each volume also containing the corresponding Latin text, and another large-format series in the same languages without the Latin text. These books were proofread and printed without knowledge of the languages. Furthermore, an Italian edition of the Bible in a small format was also decided upon. It was a memorable enterprise: they worked day and night, taking turns, for months on end. At the conclusion of the undertaking, on Christmas Eve, 1931, a copy of each edition was placed in a basket, and those books were piled up to serve as straw for Baby Jesus' cradle. This must have been the homage that pleased Him most.

THE PLUNGE INTO THE CONTINENTS

"Woe to the One Who Thinks Himself Capable"

The air was tense with expectancy. Something special was to take place in that year, 1931.

Father Alberione had begun to look with increasing concern at the world globe on his desk. By now the boys had become men, and when they came to ask his advice or receive a particular assignment, he would take the globe in his hands, turning it around again and again. As he spoke to them one by one in his paper-filled study, he sized up the qualities of each, pursuing an undisclosed end. He rejoiced at the various possibilities for world expansion that were presenting themselves to the Society of St. Paul.

One of the very first Paulines, a member of the group working in the typography school, still recalls the brief talks Father Alberione gave at Via Mazzini in Alba. Even at that time he spoke to those boys about the unimpeded expansion of their mission in the world and in the Church. When they would ask— with naïvete mixed with skepticism—whether this expansion would take place in the next generation, Father Alberione would respond smilingly that, on the contrary, it would come about very soon.

One morning in 1931, the Founder again rotated that globe on which he fixed his gaze always more often. As he did so, he informed two Pauline priests of their departure for Brazil. Thus, a new stage in the Pauline mission was beginning.

Father Alberione had developed a plan all his own for the conquest of the world through the press. More and more frequently he declared that if the mission had put down sturdy roots in Italy, it was time to think of the world beyond.

However, he explained clearly, the various Pauline missions were not to have a "missionary" aim in the usual sense. They were to continue the apostolate of the editions—no more and no less.

Another concept that he endeavored to implant in the minds of his sons was that of Christian universality. He wished his boys to stop thinking according to geographical limitations and open themselves to the immense ocean of human needs. A logical corollary to this way of thinking was complete readiness to adapt to the most different nations, customs and climes. Theirs was to be a total availability that continually recalled the strong and solemn vocation of this new undertaking in the Church: the service of God's word by means of the press through religious consecration.

News that expansion into other nations was beginning passed through the masculine and feminine communities of Alba and Rome like an electric shock. This doubled the responsibility of the members in Italy and made them more aware that sooner or later each of them should be capable of following the St. Paul "pioneers" of Brazil. But this new situation also doubled the responsibility of everyone— Mother Thecla included—who had the duty of forming personnel to carry on this little-known mission and of finding new vocations to respond to rapidly multiplying needs.

The two Pauline priests arrived in São Paulo, Brazil, on August 20, 1931. It was the same date that the Pauline mission had first begun, seventeen years before. A few days after their arrival, the priests received a letter from Father Alberione, the text of which rapidly circulated through the various Pauline houses.

"You will spread the divine word with the press," the Founder declared. "Do not conduct a business, but a spiritual business.... Do not operate a commercial industry, but be very industrious for the salvation of souls.... Do not look for money, but for everlasting treasures.... I know you are good for nothing, but neither would I want you to believe yourselves capable of anything. I would fear this; I fear it now and will continue to fear it."

These strong words revealed the Founder's credibility and also his charism. Father Alberione never relied on human means, but "straining forward," in accord with the Pauline motto, he always trusted in the limitless power of God. He wanted his priests, too, to follow him all the way in this regard.

"None of us is capable of anything," he would repeat continually. Woe to the one who thinks himself capable."

In this letter to the first priests in Brazil, he set down some practical guidelines: "First, establish the masculine house; then the feminine, at least five minutes' walk away. To both houses associate the work of the Pauline brothers and Sister Disciples" (Pauline institutes of which we shall speak further on).

In this way the plan for the establishment of the Daughters of St. Paul in Brazil was also outlined.

On October 21 of the same year (1931), the first two sisters arrived in Brazil. Only at the beginning of the month, the senior sister, who was barely twenty-one, had made her vows in the hands of Mother Thecla in the presence of Father Alberione, who blessed her and said these unusual words to her: "You are leaving for São Paulo, Brazil. The archbishop does not want the Daughters of St. Paul there; but you will be dressed in red and yellow...."

When the sisters reached their destination, the superior of the priests' community who came to meet them put his hands to his head. "And yet I wrote to the Founder not to send you!" he exclaimed. Imagine Father Alberione listening to such advice!

I cite this episode to show the mettle to which Mother Thecla formed her daughters, that they could venture upon such an undertaking as this, which, humanly speaking, might have seemed absurd.

"And If You Had To Leave Right Away?"

Mother Thecla, who was following Father Alberione step by step, now also set herself to looking for some of her daughters whom she could prepare to undertake these great thrusts across the seas.

She prepared them with simplicity, without letting them view these voyages as a great enterprise. It was just another way of carrying out God's will, she would tell them, and the same graces and help that they had received in Italy until now would certainly be present—even multiplied—at their new destinations. There was no doubt about this: in spreading the word of God through the press in an era that devoured the printed word and had made the press "the fourth estate," the mission of the Daughters of St. Paul was very modern, always up-to-date and providential.

Mother Thecla prepared her sisters, going with them still more often on their various rounds of diffusion, with a modesty and humility that never weighed upon them.

The first Daughter of St. Paul destined for the United States recalls that right during this time of preparation Mother Thecla accompanied her on a visit to the homes of the region of Asti in order to spread the word of God. Before they met anyone, Mother Thecla expressly asked that her identity not be revealed to the pastor. Later, when they were tired from walking, Mother Thecla invited her companion to sit and rest a bit on a low wall. They conversed a little, like two good friends. Suddenly Mother Thecla asked, "Tell me — does my way of offering the book seem good to you? If there is something I'm not doing well, feel free to tell me."

Touched and confused, the sister did not know what to reply.

It was at this point that Mother Thecla unexpectedly added, "If when we return home, you were to find a telegram and had to leave at once, what would you do?"

"I'd leave, Mother Thecla. I'd leave...even though the detachment from you would cost me much."

These words were not said out of convenience or adulation. The sisters were truly attached to their superior. From the beginning there had never been a dependent, servile relationship in their encounters but rather a filial, frank and familiar one, so close that it left vivid recollections in the soul of each.

Because of this, Mother Thecla was able to count on her many generous and intelligent "pioneer" daughters for the expansion of the Pauline mission in the world. Considering the times and the difficulties of communication and correspondence, the sisters' human frailty contrasted strongly with the supernatural commitment they manifested.

A short time after this conversation with Mother Thecla, the above-mentioned sister and a companion also departed—bound for the U.S.A. It was June 17, 1932, about nine months after a Pauline priest had embarked at Naples for New York. At first the priest had encountered obstacles to his staying and working in the New York Archdiocese, but these were smoothed away about a month before the sisters' arrival, when he obtained authorization to devote himself to the apostolate of the press among the Italians.

Thus, the door might be opened to the Daughters of St. Paul, following in the footsteps of those confreres who had already established themselves in São Paulo and Porto Alegre, Brazil; and Buenos Aires, Argentina. In the years that followed, Paulines also spread out into other cities in those nations.

Mother Thecla wrote to these first sisters regularly, at least once a week. In fact, we still have the letter she sent to the sisters leaving for the United States just before they sailed from Naples in June, 1932.

"I send you my best wishes—" the letter read— "my wishes that the new land to which you will go and in which you will live may be your field of labor for holiness—your own, first of all."

She did not conceal the sacrifices and difficulties from them: "Don't be discouraged if you don't see the good you do. Most of the time people are helped through obscurity, through hidden sacrifices, instead of the fervor of a clamorous apostolate."

And in a different way she drove home the same point that Father Alberione was continually hammering on, concerning his priests: "Above all, let us try to lay aside our own ego, for this is what ruins everything. And then, certainly, the Lord will come, and with Him things will accomplish themselves, or rather, *He* will accomplish them."

Then she gave some useful and practical advice: "If you want to keep peace and charity among you, let each one be willing to take blame."

Finally, she apologized, as she always did in her letters—being the first one to give an example of profound humility: "I beg you, for the love of our Lady, to forget the examples of lack of fervor and self-sacrifice that your superior has given you. I ask your charity."

In short, the more her responsibility and prestige grew in the midst of the Daughters of St. Paul, the more Mother Thecla acknowledged her limitations and did everything in her power not to place obstacles to the realization of the Founder's charism.

Alba and Rome Compete

In the thirties, the communities of Alba and Rome competed in the recruitment of vocations and expansion of apostolic activity.

The Pauline Family grew and with it grew the necessity of making room for the members and organizing the various apostolic initiatives more efficiently.

In Alba, once a second wing had been added to the house temporarily destined for the Daughters of St. Paul, the sisters dedicated themselves more completely to study, editorial work and the distribution of publications. It was at this time that their first "Feasts of the Gospel" and "Weeks of the Press" were held. From then on, these apostolic undertakings proved very fruitful.

Early in the thirties, the sisters also intensified their distribution of *Famiglia Cristiana*, the famous Pauline periodical born on December 25, 1931, and of the magazine *La Madre di Dio*, born on August 15, 1932. It may be noted here that the widely diffused European weekly *(Famiglia Cristiana)* came into being as an undertaking of the Daughters of St. Paul; a few years later it was transferred to the masculine branch of the Pauline Family.

An historic move took place in Alba in November, 1933. The sisters transferred their residence from St. Paul's Square to Corso Piave, where a house still without window panes or electricity was under construction. Although that autumn was especially cold and rainy, Mother Thecla was exemplary as always; she encouraged the sisters to meet their practical problems by recalling that their transfer should stimulate mutual progress in charity. Notwithstanding the cold weather, the open windows, and the strong drafts, none of the sisters who took part in the adventure recalls having caught cold.

In Rome the Pauline enterprise was in full flower. By now it had put down sturdy roots in the capital, and the house had begun to support itself. In 1931, seven diocesan weeklies were being printed in the Pious Society's Roman typography.

It had been necessary to acquire a linotype and two presses.

Keeping pace with the editorial and typographical development, the diffusion apostolate had also expanded. Youths of the Pious Society could be seen at church doors on Sundays intent on offering *Il Giornalino, La Domenica Illustrata,* and various books.

Surely some people rejected their offers, but, on the whole, results were good. The boys devoted themselves to this diffusion apostolate on Sundays and holydays; on weekdays they were busily engaged in study and in the technical work of the typography.

Meanwhile, the Daughters of St. Paul reached out as far as Naples, Umbria, Abruzzi and the Marches. In general, their apostolate was well received. The work to be done increased steadily, and the sisters performed this apostolate only on foot, carrying that great load of books and magazines. Because of this, Mother Thecla did not have to think twice before she asked her daughters to learn to ride bicycles and drive cars.

At that time the notion of women drivers savored of revolutionary feminism. But Mother Thecla paid no heed to what people said. While the sisters were obtaining their licenses, Providence would send the money for the automobiles. And thus it came about. The sisters did not have to stand about, with their riding whips in their hands; they began to guide their mechanical horses soon enough.

Brand new cars, driven by young sisters, were filled up with books from the Pauline typography. As we have said, this created quite a stir in those times, but, as we have also said, the sisters were unconcerned. They dauntlessly continued to perform their apostolate.

In March, 1934, the Pious Society of St. Paul was recognized as a corporation, with its main office in Alba. This recognition gave greater possibility of movement and more flexible relationships with the governments of other nations.

Also in 1934, the Society opened a book center at Pigna Square in Rome. It was the second Pauline center of diffusion in the city, the first having been established on the Julian Way the preceding year by the Daughters of St. Paul. From that time on, the

Pauline apostolate could orientate itself more decisively toward the publishing of books. 1936 saw the release of the first four volumes from the Pauline typography in Rome, and others soon followed. Two new machines had been acquired for this purpose: another press and a cutter. The increased production for distribution through the book centers was stimulated by the increasing diffusion the Daughters of St. Paul were accomplishing in Latium, Campania and throughout central Italy.

When the "World Exposition of the Catholic Press" opened in Rome in 1936, the Pious Society of St. Paul was present. This small representation would grow always greater year by year.

In China and the Far East

Meanwhile, transfers became necessary. In 1934, for example, *Il Giornalino*, a children's weekly, was moved from Alba to Rome. As the center of Christendom, Rome was the most suitable place for the expansion of the new religious family. Already the opportunity of establishing the general government in the capital was presenting itself in broad outline.

In Alba Mother Thecla worked to sustain all the various initiatives that now reached out into other continents instead of restricting themselves to Italy alone.

One of the Society's most beautiful dreams had begun to be realized in 1934. This was the Pauline Family's entrance into China and Japan. That November the first four Pauline missionaries arrived in the Orient. Two stopped in China, while their companions continued on to Japan.

Humanly speaking, their undertaking may seem to have been a failure, but they bore witness nonetheless. The priests in China managed to acquire the essentials to set up a poor typography beneath a portico in Hankow. They began to exercise their apostolate in collaboration with six youthful Chinese volunteers, who wanted to be given a share in the enterprise. Then the small community transferred itself to Nanking, where the war with Japan took it by surprise. The Paulines had to close their house; after entrusting their possessions into the keeping of a reliable Chinese, they left the mainland for the Philippines, where other Paulines had established themselves some years before.

When they were able to return to Nanking in 1938, the missionaries were confronted with the most dreadful destruction. Their type, however, and the two presses, were found beneath the rubble, almost intact. The Paulines began again; another series of events and mishaps continued until 1949, the year Mao came into power.

The priests still managed to continue their activities, although these had to be so greatly curtailed that their life resembled life in the catacombs.

In the summer of 1952, however, the new government launched a violent campaign against the Paulines. They were accused of spying; their possessions were confiscated; they were expelled from China for life.

This digression about the work of the priests in China shows how rapidly the Pauline mission had developed during the few years that had passed since its beginning.

The seal of Christian universality that Father Alberione had imprinted upon the souls of his boys had also impressed itself in the hearts of the

young sisters. Three Daughters of St. Paul entered
China early in 1937 and shared in all the trials of
the masculine branch.

The generous availability of these young
women was really admirable. It was Mother Thecla
who had formed them, training them in the spiritual
life and in practical action. Although quiet and
unobtrusive, she was extraordinarily open to the
needs of all humanity. Her sisters were to experience
the fruits of this training later on, as they carried out
the Pauline apostolate in every continent.

In this work of forming her daughters, Mother
Thecla was always ready to exact from them the
greatest possible perfection and a faithful observance
of the rule. Although she obtained these because of
her maternal qualities, she did not hesitate to reprove
and correct the sisters whenever it was necessary.

She wished her daughters to be exact and
thorough in the performance of their duties, as she
herself was. When, for example, the monthly accounts
were sent in from a daughter house in a manner different from the one established, Mother Thecla wrote
to the sister responsible: "If next month's accounts
are still done this way, I'll send them back to you."

Since the sister continued to write up the next
month's accounts in the way she had always done
it—that is, according to her own method—the accounts did indeed come back to her. Thus, she
learned her lesson. This episode was recounted for
us by the sister herself.

This same sister was one of the little group that
set out for China in 1937. Before their departure,
Mother Thecla embraced each of them and bade them
farewell. Through another sister she also sent a
letter ahead to Naples, so they would receive it before they embarked. The letter was full of affection

and maternal encouragement. Mother Thecla especially urged the sisters to love one another, to remain faithful to their superiors and united to them, to form a community of love before all else and to strive for holiness with all their energies.

She often repeated—and inculcated in the novices and young professed sisters—that it was nothing to go to the ends of the earth, even though this was extraordinary; it was nothing to set sail for the most distant continents, even though this was praiseworthy; what counted was to live in charity towards one another so the apostolate would be more fruitful.

Without their commitment to religious perfection, their apostolate would have no effects; apostolate could only germinate from consecration, as a stream flows from the spring that is its source.

Rome continued to exercise a strong attraction on the work of Father Alberione. In 1936, the Founder decided to move definitively from Alba to the Via di Grottaperfetta in Rome. At the same time, Father Giaccardo became superior of the motherhouse in Alba; in this role he also assumed the responsibility of training new personnel for the Pauline apostolate.

Mother Thecla, too, considered it opportune to transfer the government of the Daughters of St. Paul (together with the school and novitiate) from Alba to Rome. This took place on November 11, 1936. Thus, the first house of Rome became the general motherhouse of the Daughters of St. Paul, and a new period began in the life of Mother Thecla.

Unquestionably the transfer to Rome marked a new stage in the growth of the feminine Pauline branch. Everything went smoothly, and the community of Alba matured to the point of being able to sustain the vanguard of the Pauline apostolate in the most distant continents.

In 1934, Mother Thecla had decided that her daughters should begin studying philosophy and theology. She knew that they must be educated in various areas — and not superficially — in order to succeed in the task the Founder had entrusted to them.

She rejoiced over the progress of her daughters, and it was to follow their accomplishments more closely as well as to draw strength for her task from the nearness of St. Paul and St. Peter — represented by his successor — that Mother Thecla was quick to take up residence in Rome.

From Rome she would begin her lifelong series of trips to various nations. Yet she would always have time for new undertakings. She had scarcely arrived when she organized a movement for a "Central Book Center" with the specific purpose of providing the various centers managed by the Daughters of St. Paul with information about new publications and suggestions for new initiatives in the apostolate of the press.

THE FIRST OVERSEAS JOURNEYS

Her First Transoceanic Voyage

Mother Thecla had a profound understanding of Father Alberione's passion—that Christian universality of his which would be the continuing inspiration of all his undertakings.

"The Pauline Family"—the Founder once declared—"opens itself to the whole world.... Every problem and event is evaluated in the light of the Gospel.... Christ must be carried in the hearts of all peoples...."

This ideal of Father Alberione's welled up from the springs of his boundless admiration for St. Paul, whom he pointed out as the "saint of universality." The Founder always said that his intimacy with St. Paul began with his study and meditation of the Letter to the Romans. For him, Paul was truly "the Apostle." Hence: "Every apostolate and every apostle must draw inspiration from him."

The same universal spirit that animated St. Paul in evangelizing the pagan world of his times was instilled by Father Alberione in his young men, and also in Mother Thecla, so that she would share it with her daughters. This explains why the Daughters of St. Paul showed not the slightest hesitation when the time came to cross oceans and establish themselves in other lands. "Working in one nation or another is like working in various rooms off the same hallway...to go to another nation is like changing rooms" — thus declared Mother Thecla.

Her first transoceanic voyage was undertaken in order to visit the communities of the two Americas. Setting out from Genoa on March 26, 1936, she arrived thirteen days later in Rio de Janeiro. Her first stop was São Paulo. The pioneer Daughters of St. Paul in Brazil had first been guests of Mother Cabrini's sisters, who were completely at home in the Americas and carried out the very fruitful apostolate and initiatives that the "saint of the immigrants" had personally developed in the first twenty years of our century.

Like Mother Cabrini, Mother Thecla was also to have a large number of journeys to her credit — but fortunately she would be able to use more rapid means of travel, including the airplane.

By now her sisters had put down roots in São Paulo. At first their activities had been restricted to learning the language and performing domestic duties in the house of the priests; but as time went on, other young sisters had arrived from Rome and they had been able to begin diffusion in the various sectors of that immense city. They had thus been able to look for larger living quarters and even to open a book center. Two years before Mother Thecla's arrival, the sisters had set up a small typography and had begun to print the magazine A Família Cristã on a regular monthly basis.

When she arrived, Mother Thecla realized that the sisters did not have enough working space, and she decided that they should find a larger house, situated in one of the better sections of the city. Her practicality was always inspired by love for her daughters.

Mother Thecla also visited the sisters stationed in Buenos Aires, Argentina, where the beginnings had been especially difficult. By now they were regularly printing *Il Buon Angelo*, a periodical for the religious instruction of the people.

This visit made Mother Thecla especially happy. The first Argentine candidate had received the religious habit two years before, and other aspirants had come to work enthusiastically in the apostolate of the press.

Shortly thereafter, in New York, Mother Thecla met four U.S. candidates, who were to receive the habit two years later.

The foundation of the first house in the United States had met with many obstacles. Without funds, and knowing neither the area nor the language, the Daughters of St. Paul had first performed domestic duties for the priests. Then they had found an apartment and begun diffusion among the Italian immigrants. In 1934, they had begun to perform the technical apostolate, having set up a small bindery. Mother Thecla's visit encouraged the small community, which in vast New York was truly the "little flock" of the Gospel.

The first sisters who arrived in the U.S. recall that when they were about to depart from Naples, Mother Thecla sent them with great concern a bundle of heavy woolen winter garments. The first letter these sisters had received upon arriving in New York had shown similar concern. It read, in part: "I hope you have had a good trip. Are you well? Are you happy? I think these first days must be a little hard. Write much—how you are, what you are doing, where you are staying—everything, everything.... I cannot say anything else except that I feel how far away you are, but I always keep you near."

The following year Mother Thecla decided to return to New York, since on January 1, 1937, Patrick Cardinal Hayes had entrusted some parishes to the Pauline priests, at the same time giving the Daughters of St. Paul permission to establish a convent in one of the five great boroughs of the city of New York—Staten Island.

Mother Thecla was particularly enthusiastic about life in the United States. She declared that the American people were truly generous and could develop their natural gifts in the service of the Christian message. But they had to be approached in the right way. For this reason Mother Thecla responded enthusiastically to a particular request of U.S. bishops and priests—parochial census.

When taking census, the Daughters of St. Paul visited all the families in a particular area, no matter what their faith—Catholic, Protestant or non-Christian. For each Catholic family, a census card was filled out and given in to the parish. Mother Thecla was pleased because this house-to-house census gave the sisters a chance to approach these families, which had often strayed far from the Christian life, and to bring them back to the Church. The Daughters of St. Paul offered suitable books to these families and left an inspiring leaflet with each one.

This apostolate was so successful that Mother Thecla once wrote: "Census-taking accomplishes good, and it is well to do it even at the cost of sacrifice."

She never failed to remind her sisters, either in person when she returned to New York, or by letter, of the emotion she felt knowing how many people were still far removed from knowledge of the word of God.

The "Decalogue of Quickness"

"If we were many, how much more good we could do to all these people!"

This was a continual torment that gnawed at Mother Thecla after every trip. The ship bringing her back from New York arrived at Naples in early May, 1937. It would be a long time before she could set foot on a deck again. Necessity was about to halt her travels; World War II already loomed on the horizon. The years 1937 to 1945 would be the most painful for her; inability to communicate directly with her sisters would cost her many days of anguish. She could carry on a regular correspondence with some but not with all, and whatever happened in any part of the world alarmed her at once.

"What will become of our house? What will the sisters do?" she would repeat to her closest collaborators. Then she would close herself in her office and write letter upon letter, taking advantage of even the briefest moments of her arduous day. She sought to be most prompt in replying to everyone, even if briefly; she wished all her sisters to have a concrete token of her nearness and motherly presence.

Many incidents have been recorded.

"While the Second World War was raging," a sister recalls, "Mother Thecla kept in touch with us regularly by mail. She was always concerned about our health. She urged us to study the language well [this sister was stationed in China] and to insert ourselves gradually into our new Chinese environment so as to be in a better position to carry out our apostolate. I must mention her promptness in answering our letters. During the long years of the war we were deprived of news. We could not communicate with her directly, nor could she with us. So she endeavored to send her letters to us through the United States, whenever communication with the U.S.A. was possible."

When communication between Italy and the Far East was re-established, this sister could declare that none of her letters had gone unanswered. "She was so exact and concise that she could give a clear, brief reply to the most lengthy explanations, no matter what they concerned. Mother Thecla was very sensitive to the swift passage of time, to the urgency of her duties and to the very real need for hard work and total utilization of the present moment so that one's whole being would be given to the glory of God and the propagation of His word."

Her "Decalogue of Quickness" is famous. This is the "decalogue," which was sent to her daughters one year as a Christmas gift:

1. Be quick in dealing with superiors and fellow sisters.

2. Be quick on the telephone and in the parlor. Let your conversations be brief and edifying.

3. Be brief in correspondence. Long letters are equivalent to long conversations.

4. Be quick in carrying out directives.

5. Be quick in leaving one place for another, without much regret and sadness.

6. Be quick in your farewells when departing and your greetings when arriving.

7. Be quick in the book centers and in the distribution of films.

8. Be quick in performing your duties.

9. Be quick in your way of acting. Have religious dignity always, but without affectation.

10. Be quick in the confessional. Hold no long conversations; give a simple and clear explanation of what is necessary and nothing else.

THE WAR YEARS

The "Slap" of Our Lady

In 1939, as the war began, the Daughters of St. Paul were already scattered in several parts of the world. They had been in Brazil since October, 1931; in Argentina since December of the same year; in the United States since mid-1932; in France since June, 1935; and in China since the beginning of 1937.

Obliged to leave China when war with Japan broke out, the sisters took refuge in Delhi, India. Then they embarked for Lipa, in the Philippines, where they continued to propagate God's word through the press. But 1941 to 1945 in the Philippines were years fraught with flights and terror. At one point Lipa City was completely destroyed, and the house in which the sisters had been staying — from which they had launched a promising series of apostolic initiatives — was razed to the ground by bombs.

It is difficult to summarize everything that befell the young Congregation during those years.

First, a brief note about the foundation in France: when the pioneer sisters had set out for Lyons, Father Alberione had encouraged them thus: "It does not matter if you do not have much education and do not know the language; God will take care of everything."

The war plunged the sisters in France into so many difficulties that the Italian consulate urged them to come away. They, however, chose to remain in their mission field.

The indescribable anxiety and sorrow Mother Thecla felt because of reduced communications with her sisters in other lands led her to find every possible means of keeping in touch. She prayed constantly for her daughters' safety.

Decisively, Father Alberione made a vow: after the war he would construct a large shrine in honor of Mary, Queen of Apostles, if the Blessed Mother would protect and spare from death all the members of the Pauline Family scattered throughout the world, Italy included. That petition was to be granted, and at the end of the conflict, construction of the shrine would begin in the midst of financial and other difficulties, which Mother Thecla greatly helped to overcome through the intelligent and generous labors of the sisters.

Many were the adventures of the war years, and vivid were the accounts of them.

It was feared that Rome, too, would be bombed. Mother Thecla encouraged her daughters by telling them, "The Blessed Mother will slap the bombs away; nothing will happen." She was confident because of the vow made by the Founder.

One day the sisters' convent was surrounded by armed German soldiers.

The sisters had taken refuge in their bomb shelter, in which there were also some Italian soldiers the Germans were seeking. "Save yourselves!" Mother Thecla had told those soldiers, and she had helped them reach the shelter.

The Germans set up a machine gun at the entrance to the shelter. A brave sister came forward to intervene, and when Mother Thecla realized that one of the priests, too, was about to place himself in danger, she herself came forward and stood in front of the German soldiers, as if to say, "Now strike; shoot at me."

As midday approached, she had calmed them all — foes and friends alike. Then she prepared food and had it brought to everyone. By acting as she did, Mother Thecla saved not only her sisters, but also a number of boys and soldiers who were being hunted to the death.

During this period the sisters acquired a plot of land adjacent to their house. The large hall on this land served as a kindergarten and chapel for the people of the Volpine Hill. Later it became a movie hall.

While the building was serving as a movie hall, it inexplicably caught fire, and a few people were killed or injured. In the midst of so much sorrow, Mother Thecla maternally devoted herself to helping the stricken families. She did so in such a way that all the injured received help and no one lacked food or anything else.

During the war, Mother Thecla also showed herself expert in first aid. She even asked that basins of water be kept handy on every table in the house during the bombing raids, for she had heard that asphyxiation from gas could be prevented by breathing through a wet cloth.

For each possible occurrence, there was a sister assigned to warn the community.

German soldiers were also won over by the kindness of Mother Thecla. One day two of them presented themselves and asked to make an inspection of the house, suspecting that some men they were looking for were being harbored. Mother

Thecla herself accompanied the soldiers through the various rooms so they could verify that only sisters lived there. When the two soldiers asked to be put up for the night, she had a sleeping place prepared for them in the parlor. In the end, they did not stay, but by now Mother Thecla had won the trust and good will of their commanding officers — so much so that when the tide of the war turned, these German officers advised her about some precautions to take. She also asked them to look after the safety of her sisters in Viterbo and Bologna. The captain solemnly promised that not even a hair of the sisters' heads would be touched — and so it was.

Mother Thecla suffered from the enmity between the opposing sides. For her, there were no enemy soldiers among them; there were only poor boys who had to obey orders from above, who suffered hunger and thirst among other things and spent whole days without a moment's rest.

"They are all sons of God," she would say. "Everyone of them, too, has a soul, and how much our Lord has done for each!"

Fired by this conviction, she saved many soldiers from danger, hunger and cold. Food was scarce, but she always managed to find something for them; in the sacks destined for them had to be placed a ten days' supply of bread and other things that she had prepared. Probably the soldiers would return after eight days....

"Give it, give it," she would say to her sisters. "The Lord will provide."

Many disbanded soldiers found Mother Thecla a safe refuge. They came for provisions for themselves and their companions, and every time there was some little surprise for them: now, a bottle of liquor to help them get warm; now, a blanket; now, scarves, sweets or even clothing to help them disguise themselves.

The sisters kept telling Mother Thecla that instead of soldiers some of these men might be civilians taking advantage of the situation. These comments displeased her, for she could not believe that people would engage in such deception. And then, they were so sincere with her!

Nevertheless, on one occasion two "soldiers" were followed by one of the sisters, who saw clearly that at least one of them was not a soldier at all; he had simply teamed up with the other man in order to partake of that providential goodness. This civilian never showed up again, but neither did his companion return for such a long time that the sisters began to think that he, too, must have been an impostor.

One day, however, he did come back, though very timidly. He told Mother Thecla, "I saw the sister following me. Although she doubted my authenticity, I had to take another route because I can't let myself be followed. I'm afraid that the others would ruin everything if they found out about this. I'm at _____ (and he named the place). It's only right that you should know; but I repeat, I can't say this to all the sisters because I can't reveal the hiding place of the others."

Mother Thecla was very pleased by this explanation, which typified the great difficulties of that period, a period in which consciences were disturbed and the satisfaction of the most basic human needs was one of the hardest of tasks. Indirectly this was a lesson for the less confident sisters, who from then on would always rally to the support of Mother Thecla whenever confusing or difficult situations arose.

This is an example of one such situation: A band of soldiers was hidden in a cave not far from the sisters' convent. Every week one of them would run the risk of coming to Mother Thecla, who received him as a brother, or rather as a son, and gave him everything she had managed to gather together: food, clothing, blankets, cigarettes and matches....

And to the supply of provisions she did not fail to add some uplifting leaflets to read.

She came to the aid of everyone, including the men working around the convent and their families, for she knew well the poverty that prevailed in those times.

One of these laborers, a father of thirteen, can testify to this. In the midst of her many worries, Mother Thecla always managed to find time to inquire about his health and that of his family. And she was also concerned that the children grow up good and honest.

This had all begun one day when the laborer's company had sent him to do some work for the Daughters of St. Paul, and one of the sisters had asked him at noontime, "Aren't you going to lunch?"

The workman had replied that because of the food rationing he never ate at noon, in order to give that small portion to his children.

"Wait here five minutes," the sister said. "I'll bring you some soup and something else."

Soon after that Mother Thecla knew the whole story, met the workman, and did everything in her power to improve the living conditions of his family.

The Benedictines of Cassino Sheltered
by Mother Thecla

"Mother Thecla reached out to everyone:
rich and poor, learned and unlearned, small and
great. She had words of encouragement and faith
for all. Towards everyone she showed rare and immense charity, delicate and great compassion, in
times when it was very difficult to give any financial
help at all." Thus testifies the Mother Abbess of the
Benedictine Sisters of Cassino.

At a point when the war was raging most
fiercely, there was no hope for the liberation of
Cassino and Montecassino. In October, 1943, the
Father Abbot, Dom Diamare, had the Benedictine
Nuns climb aboard whatever trucks he was able to
borrow and flee to Rome—to the Basilica of St. Paul.
One morning a monk from the basilica came to Mother
Thecla to ask whether she could accomodate some
Benedictines from Cassino, who were seeking shelter
because their convent was threatened with destruc-
tion.

Right at that time, Mother Thecla had sent the
younger aspirants home, for fear that the war would
have kept them separated from their parents for a
long period, exciting anxiety on the part of both.

"In this way," she replied to the monk, "we
have a section of the house available. By all means,
let them come. We will adapt to the situation."

"And how many can you accomodate?" asked
the monk.

"They have already suffered enough in having
to abandon their convent," replied Mother Thecla
at once. "They are cloistered sisters, and to suffer
further separation would be a greater sorrow still.
If they can adapt themselves, let all of them come

here with us. They will share our refectory and
chapel. During the day they can gather in this room"
—she indicated it—"and pray and work according to
their customs. And of course, whenever they wish
to go to chapel to recite their Office, they may do so."

Thus, the approximately thirty sisters of the
Benedictine convent of Cassino entered the house
of the Daughters of St. Paul. Mother Thecla was the
first to greet them. "I welcome you as if you were
my own daughters," she said, "and I ask the Lord
that whatever I do for you may be repaid to all my
daughters scattered throughout the world who find
themselves in the same situation as yours."

A large dormitory, various smaller rooms for
the more seriously ailing, and a work room were
placed at the disposition of the new guests by Mother
Thecla. As she had said, the refectory was to be
shared, in order to keep up the sisters' spirits—
for the news arriving was more alarming every day
in regard both to Cassino and Montecassino.

Mother Thecla never manifested any regrets
about the presence of the Benedictines. She was the
first one to try to keep them happy. She redoubled
her care and diligence to see to it that they never
lacked what was necessary.

Surely, times were hard. For example, some
Daughters of St. Paul, following Mother Thecla's
suggestion, managed to make a trip to Bolsena under
cover of night to obtain potatoes, chestnuts and
other food, which was fraternally shared with the
new community.

Mother Thecla well knew what spirits they
were in, exiled as they were and far from their
convent. For this reason, she prevailed upon her
daughters from time to time to prepare some entertainment in order to cheer the guests.

In the shelter during the air raid alerts, Mother Thecla always encouraged the Benedictines. The thought of their convent was fixed in their minds; when the bombers thundered overhead they themselves admitted that they pressed close about Mother Thecla, who showed admirable self-control and serenity.

"Have faith," she would say. "Let us be good and as prudent as possible. But, even more, let us have faith in the pact made with our Lady; at the end of the war, we will begin to build the votive shrine to the Queen of Apostles."

And she would repeat what she also told her daughters: "If our Lady sees a bomb dropping toward us, she will slap it away, into the field. Let us have faith."

One day the news came that Cassino and Montecassino had been destroyed. There was no more hope.

Mother Thecla read the suffering in the faces of the Benedictines. To be exiles with the hope of returning home was a sorrow, yes, but yet bearable. Now that their home had been destroyed, their exile would be torture.

"Don't worry," she encouraged them. "Our house is God's, and therefore yours, too. No one is going to tell you to leave, nor will I let you be sent to other convents. The Lord will provide for us because we trust Him!"

One day the Benedictine prioress burst into tears as she crossed the threshold of the refectory. "We feel ashamed to come into this refectory and eat your sisters bread!" she sobbed.

At first Mother Thecla gave her a serious look. Then she smiled and said, "Don't talk that way any more. This house is God's, not ours. We're happy to have you here. Let's leave it all up to Him. Courage, Mother!"

Meanwhile, a number of houses in the vicinity —which had been occupied by soldiers—were now left empty as the American troops pressed northward. The Benedictines suggested to their superiors that they move into one of these villas which was within view of the Daughters of St. Paul convent.

When informed of this wish, Mother Thecla replied at once, "Surely. But the beginning will be hard. I know your conditions and will continue to help you. I remember our own beginnings—our sacrifices, our poverty. But the trust in God that sustained us will be your support, too."

It was already August, and Mother Thecla was eager to have the Benedictines celebrate the feast of the Assumption together with the Daughters of St. Paul. And so it was not until August 18 that the nuns took possession of their new home. Of course, they found nothing in the villa; plates, glassware, linens, clothing and foodstuffs were supplied by the Daughters of St. Paul. Mother Thecla often went to visit the Benedictines, and whenever the burden of her occupations prevented her from doing this she sent her sisters to inquire about their health and morale. She did not want them to feel ill at ease in asking for anything they might need.

"One day," relates the mother prioress, "she surprised us by sending a little pig—in fact, she came in person to tell us, 'Now, fatten it up as best you can, and you will have sausage, too.' She also presented us with a little watchdog, saying, 'Your house is isolated and someone might come to disturb you.'"

In this way the Benedictines spent a few years in their new home, always in a very close relationship with the Daughters of St. Paul. In fact, the window of Mother Thecla's office directly faced the nuns' villa, and she often said to them, "When I enter my office, my thoughts and my gaze fix themselves on you. I ask God to bless you, and I pray for all of you."

Mother Thecla's ardent and simple spirituality had taken hold of these sisters, too, and their candidates as well. One of these, who became a novice during the community's stay in the villa, recalls, "I had been so impressed by the charity of Mother Thecla that I decided to take the name 'Sister Thecla' when I made my religious investiture. She herself came to celebrate the occasion with us and rejoice over her 'twin.'"

APPROVAL OF THE "SISTERS OF THE PRESS"

Let Us Motorize To Accomplish More

Laudatory approbation, including the decree and the first papal approval of the constitutions of the Daughters of St. Paul, took place on December 13, 1943. The war was still raging, and the Congregation was still suffering from many difficulties, but surely the approbation of the constitutions was a very important step.

By this time the new feminine religious institute was known in many parts of Italy and in some other lands, not only by people in ecclesiastical circles but also by the civic and lay world, because of the strong ties the sisters had established everywhere.

Most people were at first surprised and then impressed by this new apostolate. Even in times so near our own, it was truly extraordinary to see sisters who did not dedicate themselves to teaching, to the care of orphans or the subnormal, to the care of the infirm and elderly or to other charitable activities — sisters who, instead, ran printing presses and bound books, which they distributed together with magazines. Only a few acquaintances, however, knew the sacrifices and fatigue that this work entailed. These people could not help but observe and eventually admire sisters who would spend weeks at a time far from their convents, carrying a load of books from house to house, sometimes having to brave rude responses and irreverent remarks or the most bitter incomprehension — sisters who had been driven away as if they were peddlers and yet persevered. The Congregation was all the more admired because all this was happening in a period in which the press had become a vehicle of materialistic ideas and morally objectionable writings.

There were sisters who offered their lives "to make reparation with a life of total sacrifice for the harm caused by evil publications." Youthful energy alone could not explain these sisters' enthusiasm. They felt the beauty of their apostolate as if God Himself had directly inspired each of them with it. In each sister could be discovered Mother Thecla's handiwork, the result of her carving and chiseling. She had taken advantage of every opportunity to strengthen in her daughters the ideal of their vocation. This was especially true after the constitutions approved by the Church gave a particular character to their religious consecration and increased personal and collective responsibility. From that time on, the institute would be the Church for them. To obey the constitutions was to obey the Church and to participate directly in the Church's saving mission.

This called for an upsurge of quality, a more total commitment, a more vital rapport among the members of the Congregation, a greater love. Keeping firm the bonds of charity among her sisters was Mother Thecla's daily concern. She paid no heed to time or expense when it was a matter of maintaining the closest ties with them.

Mother Thecla strengthened the ties of love with her daughters through acts of concrete sharing in their life. She wanted her sisters to be well cared

for and to always enjoy good health, for she knew the
hard life they had to lead. And she quickly saw ways
of lightening their work. Thus, when Father Alberione began to stress organized distribution of the
publications of the Society of St. Paul and the necessity of contacting various institutions on a nation-
wide basis in order to penetrate more deeply into
every district in which the Daughters of St. Paul were
already established, Mother Thecla, well knowing the
difficulties of her daughters' work, actuated an idea —
to "motorize" the sisters so they could reach more
institutions in a brief period of time.

She personally contacted a motorcycle manu-
facturing firm and asked whether they could produce a model on which two sisters could travel with
bags of books. This amazing innovation may even
have surprised some people, but Mother Thecla
would repeat, "Let us motorize the sisters, so they
may go about doing good."

We have already seen how inclined she was
to use the most rapid means of communication. Hers
was a practical mentality, open to the useful innovations of progress. And her eagerness was caught
by the sisters.

The Long Journeys Are Resumed

In December, 1945, Mother Thecla set out on
the third in her long series of journeys, to visit the
United States and South America. On this third tour,
she was accompanied by four Daughters of St. Paul
and the Founder himself.

They arrived in New York on January 11,
1946, and spent a month visiting the houses of the
United States.

Mother Thecla had a special intuition regarding the apostolic necessities of this nation, as well as the potential of her sisters. As always, her presence gave great inspiration and encouragement.

During this visit, Mother Thecla devoted much of her attention to the sisters who carried out distribution. Diffusion was not always easy in the new continent. She urged the superiors to have special esteem and understanding for these sisters, and she also encouraged them from Italy by mail. "Have courage!" she said. "All your footsteps are counted. A sister who carries out diffusion with a supernatural spirit undergoes her purgatory now, as the Founder has told us. Courage! Go ahead!"

In order to save time, Mother Thecla took a plane from New York to visit the houses of São Paulo and Porto Alegre, Brazil. A month later, she arrived in Argentina, to visit the convents of Buenos Aires, Rosario and Santa Fé. She then returned to Brazil and New York.

Ship was the means of travel Mother Thecla chose for her return to Italy. She was accompanied by a Brazilian sister who would be trained to deal with Latin America's apostolic needs.

Mother Thecla was to return to America a few years later, on her way back from a visit to the Philippines and Japan.

"Sixteen-millimeter Apostolate"

In those years immediately following the war, the activity of the Daughters of St. Paul was intense. Publication of the well-known weekly, *Famiglia Cristiana,* which had been forcibly halted during the war, was resumed in 1946. The Daughters of St. Paul began an intense drive for subscriptions. They also channeled their apostolate into various enterprises, concentrating their efforts now on one undertaking, now on another.

In many cities they organized "celebrations of the Gospel," "weeks of the press," "Marian feasts," or book fairs. Thousands and thousands of books printed and bound by the Daughters of St. Paul flowed out from Alba and Rome.

And then came the film apostolate. This has its own story in the history of the Society of St. Paul.

In 1934, American Catholics had organized the Legion of Decency to counteract immoral films, but no one had taken the initiative to produce films that positively contrasted with such productions. In 1936, the Holy Father shook the Catholic world from its slumber with the encyclical *Vigilanti cura,* in which he took a firm stand against the dangers presented by motion pictures. That was when Father Alberione decided to implement a plan he had already had in mind for years. And so, the first Pauline films came into being. One of these, *Abuna Messias* —released in 1938—was awarded a prize at the Venetian Film Festival the following year. After the production of two small films that achieved little success, the apostolate launched out into the sixteen-millimeter medium. Father Alberione had already set forth an extraordinary program: "Provide 16mm projectors for the pastors and supply them with films, the best standard-speed films that are now in circulation, so that priests can show good and safe productions to their faithful."

In December, 1948, Mother Thecla listened to a talk given by Father Cordero of the Society of St. Paul on the film apostolate, in which the sisters were not as yet engaged.

For Mother Thecla, as for many other sisters, familiarization with this cinematographic activity constituted a real revelation. She was particularly impressed by Father's words and saw the enormous potential of motion pictures. This truly could be, she thought at once, a new field of apostolate with which her daughters could actively collaborate. It would be difficult, to be sure, but it was a real mission, necessary and urgent.

Meanwhile, Father Alberione had laid down more precise guidelines for the intensification of the new endeavor; this fact was enough to convince Mother Thecla that this was the will of God, to be put into effect at any cost. In fact, she and other sisters even took part in some scenes of the color motion picture *Mary*, produced by St. Paul Films.

The film apostolate was certainly not an easy undertaking, for it presented dangers of various types besides the necessity of meeting the great expenses entailed.

Personnel had to be trained, also, and this called for much work. When the distribution of 16mm films began, the sisters had to be taught how to carry it out—checking the films' condition, making splices, registering bookings, keeping accounts, mailing and advertising. The Pauline brothers took to the road to publicize the film agencies of the Society, while the sisters did the same for the agencies entrusted to the Daughters of St. Paul.

The Founder made it clear that, above all, formative and religious films were to be programed along with the standard feature productions. The former were to include shorts that were truly and authentically catechetical. Mother Thecla became

enthusiastic about this, and even though such catechetical productions would entail quite an expense,
she did not hesitate to take the initiative of financing
the whole program. And always to give encouragement and keep personal track of the way the few
sisters entrusted with the production of the catechetical series were living and working, she herself
spent some days on location with them.

The Pauline priest who oversaw the produc-
tion of this series still recalls very clearly that Mother
Thecla was interested in everything that directly concerned her daughters. Even in him, he states, she
infused a great enthusiasm to continue the project.
And he adds, "Without Mother Thecla's help and
encouragement, I do not know whether I would have
continued in an apostolate that was so difficult and
so exacting."

Above all, Mother Thecla was concerned
about the good of her sisters. When a film could be
watched only with reservations, she wanted it to be
excluded, nor did she feel she could be lax about a
film of this kind being shown on the grounds that
knowing its content would make one better able to
advise others about it.

"This reason is often only a pretext," she
observed.

And even with regard to the press she would
tell the sisters, "Do not read all the books you distribute! There are reviews for you to read, as well as
the various aids that we send you from the main
center so that you may learn about the contents of
the books. The same is true of the films; we send you
descriptions. Rely on these. Be on guard, for the
devil is wily and finds many pretexts to lead you to
disobey in this very important matter. Be attentive!"

At a time when enthusiasm for the Congregation's new means of communication — motion pictures — was at its height, Mother Thecla was, in effect, the guardian of the Congregation's spirit. She knew only too well that unless the spirit of prayer was active and strong, the apostolate would accomplish nothing.

"How beautiful our apostolate is!" she remarked once. "Today I was speaking of exactly this: that we must always use the more modern means to do good; our constitutions, too, say this. Therefore, we must always be up-to-date in our activity, always progressing with the times.

"However," she added at once, "we must never lose our spirit of faith and prayer — and the conviction that we are good for nothing and that it is God who accomplishes things."

When the preparation of records and filmstrips was begun at Grottaferrata, near Rome, in 1954, she threw herself into it with all the zeal that was hers. One time the sister who accompanied her regularly as driver and companion asked, "But, Mother Thecla, aren't filmstrips a step backwards, with their still pictures? We already have 16mm films...."

"Oh, no!" replied Mother Thecla. "This means of communication is widely used, especially in catechetics, for the picture can be held in place and explained well until everyone has understood the lesson. They are both needed. We must also think of people who do not know how to read and those who cannot afford to buy a 16mm projector. The Founder says that this is the time of the record and filmstrip."

The concreteness and practicality of Mother Thecla may be noted. According to her, the means more perfected by progress must never supplant the more humble means, for the apostolate must develop even according to the capacity of the recipients. It was necessary to keep their preparation in mind; she had had much experience regarding this during her extensive travels. Some means that seemed modest — such as still filmstrips — could produce the best results from the standpoint of apostolate.

FROM CONTINENT TO CONTINENT

"Far-eastern Spring"

In the late 1940's, four Daughters of St. Paul, who had been chosen to found the house of Tokyo, were received by Pope Pius XII in an audience exceptional for those times.

"We are going to Japan, Your Holiness," said one of the sisters, "but we know neither the language nor anything else about the land and its people."

Pius XII opened his arms in that expansive gesture characteristic of him and exclaimed, "To Japan! To Japan! How pleased I am! I bless you very much. I give you a special blessing: for the trip, for all your needs, for the language, for your interior life.... Interior life! I especially bless your interior life!"

This blessing of the Holy Father's was needed, for the young sisters would have to overcome many obstacles. The Pauline priests before them had also surmounted great difficulties following their arrival in Japan in 1934. After the interlude of the war, the priests had resumed their editorial work; in 1949, they were to initiate their radio apostolate.

The sisters arrived in Japan in 1948. Difficulty with the language kept them almost isolated until an American sister joined them near the end of the year; they then began distribution of books among

American servicemen. The generous offerings received permitted the entrance of the first Japanese candidates. And thus, the apostolate to the people of Japan could begin. In 1948, the sisters also purchased (naturally with the help of Mother Thecla) the ground on which their convent was to be built.

In the reports that reached her, Mother Thecla saw such a spirit of initiative to be channeled and directed that a visit on her part was in order.

Activity had been resumed in the Philippines, now that the sisters had rebuilt the convent destroyed in the war.

However, it was necessary for Mother Thecla to see the situation at first hand. Hence, she set out on a long voyage, together with Father Alberione.

They arrived in Manila in April, 1949. Immediately Mother Thecla set out for Lipa, where she spent more ·than a month—a visit particularly soul-stirring for all her daughters and for herself.

As already noted, it had been difficult to communicate with the sisters of the Philippines during the war. Mail could arrive only now and then, and many letters had been lost. Because of this, a very intense family climate of sisters about their mother was now established.

In great simplicity Mother Thecla provided the sisters with "spiritual injections," as was her custom when visiting the convents. She continually reminded her sisters of the purpose for which they had consecrated themselves to God. Amid apostolic activities she continued to call them back to the principal reason for their vocation, which was to become saints in order to help others do the same.

Mother Thecla's visits were pauses that restored the spirits of the sisters. During intense days of private and communitarian conversations with her daughters, she never let diversions be lacking, and in these, too, she took direct part. The sisters of various houses around the world recall their recreations with Mother Thecla—her games and magic tricks, the jokes and comic skits she planned and prepared while traveling in order to keep her daughters happy.

As always, during this visit to Lipa, Mother Thecla wished to be informed about everything. If she came to know that someone was trying to tell her only the positive and good without mentioning what could displease her, she would say, "You must tell me everything, not just what causes joy but also whatever brings sorrow."

At one point she let this expression escape her: "I know many things anyway, even if you don't tell me!" And she said it so naturally—without any affectation, as if it were an ordinary thing for her—so to encourage her daughters to say everything.

During this, her first visit to the Philippines, Mother Thecla learned that the travels of the sisters involved in distribution often took them far from the population centers, and that there were times when they could neither participate in the Mass nor receive Communion because of the scarcity of churches and the even greater shortage of priests. What should they do? Mother Thecla replied decisively, "Sacrifice your Mass and Communion, but go. These poor people never have anyone to visit them, to say a good word to them, to speak to them about God, to bring them the Gospel. Go everywhere, and be in peace."

Since at that time it was still impossible for the sisters in the Philippines to buy an automobile, the approximately fifty-mile trip from Lipa to Manila was generally made by means of public transportation, which traversed terrible roads, pitted with holes.

The sisters repeatedly suggested renting a car for their superior general in order to spare her such fatigue, but she would have none of it. "If you travel this way," she asked, "why can't I, too?" And so, during the great heat of May—the most stiflingly hot month in the Philippines, with a humidity that penetrates even into one's bones—she made all these trips with never a word of complaint. Often she would say, "It is not the Filipinos who must adapt, but you yourselves. You must take up their habits and customs, esteeming and appreciating everything."

That Mother Thecla's visit had borne fruit could be seen at the end of the year, when, on December 26, the Daughters of St. Paul received a letter from the new archbishop, who authorized them to open a house in the city of Manila, "extending best wishes for the accomplishment of much good through the apostolate of the good press."

The Congregation in the Philippines now stood on firm footing. Mother Thecla, however, felt she had done very little. A sister recalls that upon her departure from the Philippines Mother Thecla left behind a note in which she thanked the sisters for having "put up with me all this time," and asked pardon for not having done all she would have wished and should have done.

Mother Thecla arrived in Tokyo with Father Alberione in mid-May. Remaining in Japan until near the end of June, she was able to observe that the Daughters of St. Paul had mastered the Japanese language and had begun to train young members for the radio apostolate. Father Alberione's presence and her own so spurred on the members of both congregations that, on the following December 25, the Society was able to make its official request for the approbation of a radio station in Tokyo.

Fifteen Vocations, Like the
Mysteries of the Rosary

The beginnings in Mexico had not been very simple, especially because of the difficulties imposed by that nation's laws. Yet the Daughters of St. Paul had already taken good steps forward since their arrival in Mexico City in 1948. Mother Thecla's visit served to encourage them and to resolve many difficulties.

In June, 1949, Mother Thecla journeyed from Mexico to New York, where the apostolate of the Daughters of St. Paul had expanded much since her last visit. The sisters had printed and diffused thousands of copies of saints' lives, many Gospels and pamphlets and an infinitude of leaflets. In the morning they would go out to distribute books, while in the late afternoon and evening they would devote themselves to the "technical apostolate"—as they called it—the manual work of printing and binding. They also made the most of every opportunity to display their books in schools and colleges. The need for a new and larger home being urgent, they had found one in Derby, N.Y.

Derby became the novitiate house and house of formation for the Daughters of St. Paul of the United States. Mother Thecla had urged and approved this new location, which would permit the training of many more young people for the apostolate of the press. Visiting the convents of her daughters, she could see firsthand how much apostolate there was to be carried out and how few candidates had been found.

Maternally she spurred on the sisters who went out for distribution. "Even when the sisters who propagate God's word do not have material success," she would say, "they do have spiritual success, which counts more. The first apostolate of those engaged in diffusion is that of good example."

And she added, "Your distribution might bear few material fruits and many more of the spiritual. Have faith."

When the first books produced by her daughters in the United States arrived in Rome, she wrote at once: "I received the books; they are beautiful. You are already accomplishing much." And she continued, "I am pleased that the book center is doing well." Then she asked, "Did you go to that exhibit? Even where you do not distribute much, you at least do good to the people with whom you come in contact. I pray that you can do much good for them."

This was her great longing—to do much good to souls. For this reason, Mother Thecla always desired new candidates.

One sister recalls a time that she and Mother Thecla discussed the scarcity of vocations and the necessity of praying for them. Suddenly Mother Thecla turned toward the sister and declared decisively and resolutely, "We have to ask for them, ask them of the Blessed Mother with faith. Let us ask her to send us twelve vocations this month—twelve, like the apostles. Tell the other sisters, too, and have faith. Nothing is impossible to the Blessed Mother." And, to make a long story short, the candidates who entered during that month of May were not twelve but fifteen, just like the mysteries of the rosary.

After one visit to the U.S.A., Mother Thecla wrote to her daughters in America, "I know that the aspirants are running the machines and I am so pleased. Look for new candidates. The Blessed Mother is obliged to send them, since we have

promised her the Queen of Apostles shrine. Let us
have great trust in our most holy Mother."

When returning from the United States in July,
1949, Mother Thecla had occasion to stop in Portugal
to visit the shrine of Our Lady of Fatima. This was a
great joy to her. When she went to the Cova da Iria,
she asked for hundreds of candidates to meet the
needs of the Pauline apostolate throughout the world.
Those who accompanied her remember the simplicity and fervor with which she prayed at the
shrine. She remained entranced, as it were, absorbed in a wonderful conversation with the "holy
Madonna."

"They Never Tell Us Superiors Our Defects"

After her return from America, Mother Thecla
remained in Italy only through July and August in
order to weather the heat. At the end of September
she set out upon another journey, the fifth in the
series, to visit the convents of France and Spain.

It has already been noted that the sisters in
France had chosen to remain in their mission field
of Lyons notwithstanding the advice of the Italian
consulate to return to their homeland because of
the difficulties of the war. Only in 1948 had these
sisters been able to acquire their own home. At once
they began to foster vocations, to hold their first
"feasts of the Gospel" and to print their first booklets
for children.

It was now time to open a book center. The
sisters had already sounded out possibilities, and
during Mother Thecla's visit the concrete opportunity presented itself. Meanwhile, in March, 1948,
two Daughters of St. Paul from Lyons had arrived in
Marseilles.

They were difficult, those early years in Marseilles, but the sisters persevered so tenaciously that upon Mother Thecla's arrival it was decided to open a book center there.

Plans were also made to open a house in the French capital.

Mother Thecla continued on to Spain, to visit the houses of Barcellona and Valencia. Upon her suggestion it was decided to begin carrying out the typographical apostolate in Barcellona and to open a center of diffusion there, while the possibility of opening a book center in Valencia had already presented itself.

These visits to the houses of France, Spain and Italy constitute a complete chapter in the life of Mother Thecla. As she traveled, whether by train or by car, she and her companion prayed for the good outcome of the visit. "We have such great needs, that the Lord will help us," she would say.

Then, after the visit, she would show herself satisfied and would say with simplicity, "See how good the Lord is, how much He loves His spouses! In every city we go to, we have a house to welcome us. Not even a queen has this possibility."

Regarding this particular trip and the subsequent one to France in July, 1952, the sister-driver recalls some details that sketch the personality and generous spirit of Mother Thecla.

The mother general showed maternal concern and foresight in planning these trips. Ready for any eventuality, she always took along a first-aid kit and even a little pocket flashlight. More than once this little flashlight proved its usefulness when an unforeseen accident befell the car.

Every now and then, Mother Thecla would pop a caramel into her companion's mouth. "You are

working, and you need it," she would say. "Instead,
I'm only being transported."

And then she would ask, "Do you feel well?
When you need something, just tell me, and we'll
open up our store."

The "store" was a basket of food that she had
carefully prepared for all her guests in the car.

Although she herself did not drive, Mother
Thecla would help the driver with clear directions.
Her companion recalls, "It did not seem that I was
driving the mother general, but just a simple sister—
she was so kind and warm-hearted."

This same sister speaks of Mother Thecla's
custom—which has already been mentioned—of
praying during the trip for the visit's good outcome.
Yet she had the discernment to prevent weariness by
interspersing the prayers with hymns or with some
religious story, the reading of a passage of the Gospel
or the narration of an apostolic incident told her by
the sisters. When it was a feast day, vespers were
chanted in the car, and if the journey took place
during a novena, even in the auto Mother Thecla
kept the schedule "in rhythm with the house of
Rome" as much as possible.

She used everything as a means of elevating
herself. Nature gave her much inspiration in this
regard. Watching a tossing sea, she would conclude,
"After the storm, calm will return. It is this way
in our lives, too. We overcome our difficulties with
God's help and peace returns—tranquility to the
very depths of one's soul."

The same sister-driver relates the following
personal incident:

"Sometimes I happened to receive some correction from her that left me a little offended. But
always at our next meeting she would smile and look

at me with those penetrating eyes of hers, almost as
if she wished to say, 'Do you hold a grudge?' At other
times, instead, she would tell me openly, 'I correct
you because I love you, because I want you to be a
saint. It would be a bad sign if I had to put on white
gloves in order to tell you things. Go ahead. Be in
peace and become holy.'"

Sometimes it would happen that this same
sister felt bound to call something to Mother Thecla's
attention, taking a sort of risk.... After all, Mother
Thecla was her superior.

This happened during a visit to a house in
France. When Mother Thecla arrived, two sisters
were out performing their apostolate, and therefore
the superior telephoned them, so that they, too,
would come to greet the mother general. As soon as
one of these sisters saw Mother Thecla, she ran up
and took her hand, kissing it with great enthusiasm.
However, Mother Thecla withdrew her hand at
once, indicating that she did not really care for
this type of greeting. The sister was hurt, and her
expression showed it. "She remained sad most of
the day," noted the sister-driver.

Having turned at once to greet the second
sister, Mother Thecla had not seen the reaction of
the first. Thus, for her this was the end of the incident, but not so for the sister-driver, who had wit-
nessed the sister's disappointment as she withdrew
to the sidelines.

Mother Thecla's companion wanted to tell
her about this, but at first she did not dare. Finally,
taking all her courage "in four hands" she said,
"Mother Thecla, you didn't let that sister kiss your
hand, and the poor thing felt hurt. Calmly let her
kiss your hand without resisting.... This may help
you to approach those who do not know you well and

those who do not dare approach you, because at first sight you inspire awe."

For an instant Mother Thecla remained speechless; then immediately she replied, "I am truly pleased that you called this to my attention; I wasn't aware of it at all. You know, I don't like to have people kiss my hand, but if this will make it easier for the sisters to approach me, I will allow it without objection. It's a pity that no one ever tells us superiors our defects, even though they see them. They are afraid to tell us, and so we never correct ourselves. You really pleased me by telling me this. *Deo gratias!* Every time you see something that isn't as it should be, tell me."

This reply is an expression of genuine humility and charity.

However, the awe that Mother Thecla could arouse upon first acquaintance quickly vanished during recreation periods. Her "store"—besides containing the foodstuffs and first-aid kit for her automobile trips—also held games of various types, tricks that only she and her driver knew how to play. It has already been noted how effective these were.

In fact, Mother Thecla joked that she and her driver were "associated artists." Only the two of them performed the more complicated tricks, but when another sister would be able to help, Mother Thecla preferred to choose the more timid, the one who seemed to her to be the most bashful. Thus, the games served to entertain the sisters and make them happy, but also to create a relaxed, family atmosphere.

And yet, when Mother Thecla was playing these games with the sisters, she was always very tired, not only from her travels but also from the preoccupations that certainly were not lacking during these visits to the convents. But she knew how to make the very most of the time she had for visiting the sisters. Indeed, since she often brought from the motherhouse a sister who had specialized in various techniques of the apostolate, she saw to it that no one would lack the chance to receive this instruction, and she herself, with great simplicity and ease, would take the place of a sister serving in the book center or give her help to the sister-cook according to the necessity.

In this swift change of roles she also had a chance to appraise her sisters' health and check on the sufficiency of their nourishment. To some she urged, "Follow the cure prescribed for you; you will work again when you are well. Be happy and content and try to recover completely."

SOWING AND REAPING

"I Want Valiant Women"

The joyous appearance and temperament of
Mother Thecla stemmed from the ever greater
familiarity with which she lived in the presence of
God. Her recollection was truly impressive. During
conversations she would often look at the crucifix. So
also while traveling, when there could be so many
distractions and a thousand excuses could be found to
interrupt the regular practices of piety and interior
reflections.

Just how much the presence of God had taken
root in her is shown by a fact that a sister recounts as
having taken place in Rome in 1950. Because of a
rather serious and painful situation, Mother Thecla
was reproved by the Founder in the presence of
the community. She felt all the pain of this rebuke,
and tears welled up in her eyes. "However," states
the sister, "what impressed us was that she never
uttered a word of complaint or defense, neither then
nor later. Instead, as soon as possible, she gathered
all the professed sisters and said with her usual
calm: 'Let us thank God for everything the Founder
has told us. We will have a novena of Masses celebrated in thanksgiving, and let there be no comments made on the subject. All things are permitted
by God; we are to bow our heads and do His will.'"

After this statement, two sisters followed Mother Thecla into her office and said, "Mother Thecla, what courage you have—to be grateful to God for this trial!"

And she promptly and serenely replied: "Certainly! We must thank God for saying these things to us so clearly. Remember: this is how we must do things!"

Truly she acted as one completely dedicated to God. During the spiritual exercises of 1951, a few months after this occurrence, she wrote the following in her personal notebook: "Embrace renunciation even to the point of privation, humiliation and subjection. When there is complete and utter humiliation and confidence in God, then grace enters the soul."

Mother Thecla made humiliations and obscurity the best garments of her soul. And, as a result, she succeeded in opening herself completely to the needs, demands and comfort of her spiritual daughters. The resolution she had made to embrace renunciation and obscurity, molded her character into that of a valiant woman at the service of God.

In order that this service would be constant and generous, and that the Institute would grow and be fruitful, developing without declining from the spirit of the Founder, Mother Thecla—as we have seen—undertook long and wearisome journeys.

In 1952, together with Father Alberione, she visited the convents of North America once again. This was one of her most extensive tours because the convents in South America were also visited.

The activity of the Daughters of St. Paul in Derby, which the two superiors visited, and Youngstown, Ohio, where the sisters' first book center had been opened in 1944, was chiefly directed to individual and collective distribution; but the sisters also continued the valuable activity of census-taking, with visits to homes, which provided the opportunity of making personal contact with the members of a family and leaving the appropriate book, or at least a leaflet, in each home.

On this occasion Mother Thecla and the sisters discussed the possibility of opening a house and book center in Alexandria, Louisiana. This opening took place in August of the same year—1952. They also spoke about opening a house and book center in San Antonio, Texas; February, 1953, would see the inauguration of this center. The bishops of the United States had begun to ask for the Daughters of St. Paul, and the sisters endeavored to satisfy the desires of these shepherds as far as possible.

About two years after this visit of Mother Thecla, the archbishop of Boston, Cardinal Cushing, was to invite the Daughters of St. Paul to transfer their novitiate house and technical apostolate to Boston, where they were already operating a book center.

At the end of March the Founder and Co-Foundress flew on to Canada. Mother Thecla visited her daughters in Montreal, where a house had been opened the preceding January through the encouragement and assistance of Cardinal Leger, who had always been a great supporter of the press apostolate.

While giving a very concrete talk to the sisters, Father Alberione stated: "As soon as possible, you should plan four new undertakings: film diffusion, a catechetical magazine, a novitiate house and a spacious convent adequate to the needs of the apostolate."

The sisters looked at one another to see whether the Founder was really addressing them or if he perhaps had had some "vision" of teams of

film directors, journalists and printers other than
themselves. But because he continued on the topic
with his usual concreteness and precision, there
was no room left for doubt; they had to consent,
show themselves contented and satisfied, and set
to work.

It is a fact that a few years later these planned
undertakings became realities.

Naturally, after the Founder had spoken,
Mother Thecla would always gather her daughters
together and help them see that the mountain they
must conquer was, in reality, only a tiny hill which,
yes, did present some difficulty but would not require
rope and climbing boots for its conquest. It was only
necessary to make themselves fit, by means of faith
and good will.

In everything that concerned the carrying out of
the Founder's will, Mother Thecla was absolutely
faithful. She wanted to know his thought on any
new endeavor before setting out to accomplish it.
When a new undertaking was approved or only
desired by Father Alberione, she threw herself
into it to make it a reality and asked of her daughters
equal generosity in actualizing the Founder's ideas.

From Canada, Mother Thecla traveled to
Mexico City. The day after her departure from there
in May, 1952, the Daughters of St. Paul left for
Monterrey to open a new house in response to an
encouraging letter from the bishop, who had written:
"Come, come soon, because yours is a great apostolate!"

The sisters also established themselves in
Puebla, and a short time after their arrival there,
they received a declaration of the bishop that certainly
was one of the best testimonies to Mother Thecla's
formative action: "I am very satisfied with the work

that the Daughters of St. Paul are accomplishing here. They are like doves that pass by everywhere without fanfare and remain untainted by the evils of the world."

From Mexico Father Alberione and Mother Thecla flew to Colombia. The Daughters of St. Paul had first gone to Bogotá in April, 1948, arriving there the day after a revolution had taken place. Although the uprising had been short-lived, it had nevertheless left its traces.

It was only in January, 1949, on the occasion of the Eucharistic Congress, that the sisters made themselves known through the first national book exhibit; from that time on, they received many requests from bishops and pastors. In order to form the necessary sisters for the apostolate requested, the sisters had to begin the construction of a new house on the outskirts of the city. The inauguration of this convent took place during the visit of Mother Thecla. One month prior to her arrival in Bogotá, a film agency had also been opened. June, 1949, had seen the inauguration of a house of formation in Manizales, and the house of Barranquilla had been established in March, 1951.

Much To Plan and Do

After Colombia, Mother Thecla stopped over in Chile. Here, the Daughters of St. Paul had arrived in March, 1948, to establish a house at Valparaíso, where they found themselves in a rather precarious situation. When Mother Thecla arrived, she saw to it that more ample living quarters were provided for the community of sisters. She also saw the possibility of opening a house in Santiago, in spite of the country's economic and social difficulties. This was achieved in September, 1952.

The next stop was Buenos Aires, where, on June 16, 1951, the Argentine primate had solemnly inaugurated the church dedicated to St. Paul and where by now the activity of the sisters was intense. The monthly magazine, *Famiglia Cristiana,* begun in 1942 in Spanish, had progressed steadily in content as well as format.

Vocations were numerous in the houses of Rosario (opened in September, 1937) and Santa Fé (April, 1940); so much so that in November, 1950, the community of Santa Fé had moved into a larger house where there would be adequate facilities to establish a functional and modern book center.

Mother Thecla rejoiced over such things during this quick trip through Argentina. She had the possibility—as was her custom—to hold many personal conversations with the sisters and to hear of their difficulties and progress, gathering from these, however, the impression that the plant had taken deep roots and soon enough would bear fruit.

During the last step of the journey, in Brazil, Mother Thecla had to advise the sisters about the guidance of the great flowering of vocations that had come about in that generous land. At Porto Alegre alone, there were one hundred and fifty candidates.

At this time, Mother Thecla was further informed of the current activities in the houses of Rio de Janeiro, opened in May, 1946, of Belo Horizonte, opened in July of 1948, of Curitiba, opened in March, 1949, despite innumerable difficulties, and of Pelotas, opened in March, 1951.

Truly there was much to plan and do. The progress in Brazil had certainly been beyond all expectations, agreed Mother Thecla and the Founder as they returned to Rome in mid-June, 1952.

The "Choice" at the Chapel Entrance

The blessing given by Pius XII to the first four Daughters of St. Paul bound for Japan must have been paternal and warm indeed, for only a few years later Japanese bishops, such as those of Fukuoka, Osaka and Nagoya were asking that Pauline houses be established in their dioceses.

Right at the beginning of 1950, a book center was opened in Fukuoka, and in 1951 living quarters in Osaka were given to the sisters by the bishop himself. In addition to carrying out individual and collective distribution, the Daughters of St. Paul were actively engaged in the radio apostolate in Tokyo, where, as we have seen, some of them had been especially trained for this new technical medium of social communication.

At the beginning of 1953, the new postulants numbered seventeen, and the entire community of Tokyo, including the aspirants, had sixty members. This flourishing of vocations was the motivation for Mother Thecla's new journey to the Far East. It was the seventh in her series of long trips.

She arrived in Japan in April, 1953, and at the end of the month continued on to the Philippines, where she visited the houses of Lipa, Manila, Cebù and Davao. The Daughters of St. Paul had arrived in Cebù, the largest Philippine city after Manila, in November, 1951, and the following year they had already been able to open a book center.

At Davao, instead, Mother Thecla found only the very beginnings of a community. The house was to be opened officially on May 21, after Mother Thecla had already departed.

Located on the island of Mindanao, the house of Davao was the farthest convent from Manila. The sisters carrying out distribution had to travel from place to place by means of small, shaky boats that sometimes threatened to sink because of the weight of the books and the sisters' lack of skill in balancing.

En route back to Europe, Mother Thecla also stopped at the house of Bombay, which the Daughters of St. Paul had established in August, 1951. Having accepted their first candidates and begun distribution on an individual basis, the sisters also started to organize collective distribution during this visit of Mother Thecla.

By now the Daughters of St. Paul had many convents in Asia, and Mother Thecla's preoccupations mounted daily. It may be said that the last fifteen years of her life constituted an almost continuous passage from one plane to another in order to visit her sisters in the farthest regions of the globe. For her, "visiting the convents," meant rejoining her daughters one by one.

Looking them straight in the eye, it took little for her to understand their state of soul, for she knew each of them. Her sisters recalled how in some cases she had chosen them for the missions at the chapel entrance when they were coming out from prayer.

She would scrutinize them all, and infallibly her choice would fall on the sister best suited. Truly she had a special intuition. Then she would go to see the results of her choice and rejoice in the good her sisters were accomplishing.

She would enkindle their enthusiasm and spur them on to persevere. "Whatever you do, do it for love of God," she would say. This was the phrase that she herself had heard from Father Alberione on that famous day of her first conversation with him in the sacristy of the church of St. Damian.

"Your hearts are united to mine," she would tell her sisters, "in the love of God and of souls."

"Be always happy," she would say again. "Life passes, but what is done for the Lord remains. May we all become saints! Let us carry out God's holy will always and in all things."

And to those who were experiencing difficulties she would say, "I have great confidence that this most difficult trial will make us strong in spirit and ready in doing God's will well. Let us attach ourselves firmly to the Lord. Let us detach ourselves from creatures."

"The sign of love of God," she would repeat, "is doing His will."

This straining toward holiness which she instilled in her sisters — showing them that the simplest means of acquiring it was to die to our will to do God's will — she wanted them to ask for herself also. "Pray for me," she would say, "so I may always do God's will well and save my soul."

Mother Thecla spent the month of June, 1953, in Italy, but by mid-July she had taken to the air again, to visit the houses of Montreal, in Canada, from which she continued on to the United States, where the sisters had begun the publication of *The Family*, a monthly magazine, the preceding October. Within a few years this magazine was to have over fifty thousand subscribers.

From the United States, Mother Thecla continued on to Mexico. In August she arrived in Bogotá, where the film apostolate continued to yield promising results.

She flew on to Santiago and to Buenos Aires. In this latter city, too, the Daughters of St. Paul had initiated a film apostolate—in March, 1953. Mother Thecla was informed of an opportunity to open a convent in Tucumàn; and, indeed, on April 10 of the following year the sisters did arrive in that distant city.

The apostolate of the press was in vigorous ferment in Argentina. There was no field of information in which the Daughters of St. Paul were not involved. With her usual practicality, Mother Thecla devoted herself to seeing that this wonderful life was guided by appropriate priorities in work and apostolate.

She also visited the Brazilian convents of Rio de Janeiro, Belo Horizonte and Curitiba, along with the new house of Pelotas, where all was going well.

In early September Mother Thecla was again in Rome, but remained there only long enough to catch her breath, so to speak. By the end of October she was on the way to Spain.

The house of Barcelona was intensely involved not only in the normal distribution of the printed word but also in the film apostolate under the form of catechetical shorts and other motion pictures. As has been noted, the Daughters of St. Paul had already established themselves in Valencia, and at the end of 1952, in Valladolid as well. May, 1953, had seen the entrance of the first aspirant.

"In Barcelona and Valencia," the sister-driver relates, "Mother Thecla took a lively interest in distribution. She wanted to know how the sisters got about from place to place, since there were few means of transportation in Spain at that time. Upon learning that they always traveled by train, following very inconvenient schedules and carrying many packages of books (Mother Thecla tried to lift one of these packages and noted the effort these young sisters had to make), the Mother General made an immediate decision: 'Have someone learn to drive at once and buy a car.'"

She did not pause to wonder whether a sister behind a steering wheel in Spain at that time might cause astonishment. "You can do more good," she said, "and this way you will not ruin your health."

An Unexpected Appointment

Only shortly after her return from Spain — as can be read in the *Osservatore Romano* of September 12, 1953, Mother Thecla was named by the Sacred Congregation of Religious to be the president of FIRAS, the Italian Religious Federation for Social Assistance.

The Federation had been in existence only a short while, and this was the first time the office of the presidency had been conferred.

Mother Thecla was so taken by surprise that she wanted to be sure there hadn't been some kind of mistake. However, when she was assured that she truly had been called to make her contribution to this new organism, she gave it her generous support and began to work.

Mother Thecla was surely not one to take up a duty and put it aside. Since she knew that in all such undertakings the good of souls had to be accomplished, she threw her whole self into every activity. When time was lacking, she slept less, and when the worries mounted, she spent longer hours kneeling in prayer before the Blessed Sacrament.

In this new role, she regularly attended the general assemblies of the major superiors and occupied herself greatly with everything that this

federation of religious stood for; she understood
the importance, needs and advantages of the organization. She knew the desire of the Congregation
of Religious to help sisters become better qualified for their apostolate, and she wanted that desire
to be satisfied at any cost, even on the part of her
collaborators.

For example, during one meeting of the
federation's council, there was a discussion about
organizing a specialized summer course for sisters
who taught kindergarten. It had to be said that such
a project would present difficulties: lack of means,
places and instructors. A certain sister with a master's
degree, quite experienced in this activity, spoke
about the plan in such a negative way that the leaders
of the federation were about to lose courage over
the project, since this expert enjoyed great trust.
Not knowing what to do, they turned to their president to hear her thought.

Mother Thecla asked simply, "What does the
secretary of the Congregation of Religious say
about this?"

"He wants it very much," was the reply.

"Then we must organize this course," Mother
Thecla decided. "Let us do what is in our power;
the Lord will help us."

The course was organized, and many sisters
took part in it. It was a great success. And indeed,
other like courses were also held, to the benefit of
the sisters, even in the years that followed.

"Let Us Not Reason Humanly"

In 1955, Mother Thecla again took to the air,
bound for the Far East. This was the ninth of her
long journeys. She visited the Philippines and
Japan, returned to the Philippines and then flew

to Sydney, Australia. From Sydney she returned to Rome, stopping on the way in Bombay, India. This trip lasted from April 15 to June 2.

Here are recorded some of the events that had been taking place in the houses of the Far East.

In Tokyo, just that year, the Daughters of St. Paul had enthusiastically initiated their technical apostolate — the binding and mailing of books and periodicals. At the end of the year, following Mother Thecla's visit, the first issue of the monthly magazine *Akebono* came out. The next year the sisters would launch a new series of books with the *Life of Christ* by Fulton Sheen.

The book centers that had been opened in Fukuoka and Osaka were doing well. Regarding them, the apostolic prefect of the city of Nagoya wrote the Daughters of St. Paul, "It seems right to me that after opening a house in Tokyo you should have opened one in Osaka, since that is an important city; but after Osaka you should have opened one in Nagoya rather than Fukuoka, for Nagoya is the third city in Japan." He added, "If you would like to come right away, the house is ready." Thus, the house of Nagoya, too, was born.

Following the requests of some priests in Kobe, a book center was also to be opened in that city. Mother Thecla herself went to Kobe for the express purpose of finding the site for the house and book center. Father Alberione was also present; at a certain point on Kobe's main street, he suddenly told the sisters, "Look here and you will find it." And so it came about.

In the Philippines, Mother Thecla had a first-hand view of her daughters' apostolate in Lipa, Manila, Cebù and Davao. Everything was going in the best way possible, and there were also many

candidates. Indeed, it was at this time that the
Daughters of St. Paul also opened a convent in
Cagayan de Oro—a little city of 90,000 inhabitants,
including many Moslems, in the northern part of
Mindanao. And plans were being made for a house
in Naga City. The next year, following very active
distribution carried out by the Daughters of St.
Paul in that diocese, the archbishop began building a house for them next to the cathedral.

In the Philippines, Mother Thecla observed
how extremely difficult it was to traverse that seven-
thousand-island archipelago. She directed that from
then on the sisters should fly from place to place.
First of all—she told them—they would thus avoid
fatigue and conserve their health; then, too, they
would save time, reach more souls and work more.
This was always Mother Thecla's preoccupation
—to reach the greatest possible number of people.

The Australian visit made during this journey had a particular character. The first house in
this newest and smallest continent was personally
founded by Mother Thecla. She and the Founder
settled the first two sisters in Sydney; it was May 14,
1955, and the sisters had come from Manila. At
the end of the year the sisters succeeded in moving
into their own home, immediately launching their
apostolate with a book fair. The following year
construction of a typography began.

The two traveling superiors stopped off to
visit the houses of India before returning to Italy.
Since the first candidate had already entered, the
Founder noted how little space there was and remarked, "You need larger quarters." And he suggested that they look for a more suitable location
on which to build, so that new candidates could be
received and better formed.

Mother Thecla, who had been listening to this proposal of the Founder, let a comment escape her: "Yes, but the means are lacking."

Father Alberione looked at her seriously and replied, "And what about faith? Is it possible that one can reason so humanly?"

The sisters relate that Mother Thecla accepted the remark humbly, thanked Father Alberione, and later told them, "Did you hear what the Founder said? Let us have faith!"

This profound expression, "Let us have faith!" was her habitual refrain. Always when things were not going well she would repeat it. In her letters, too, she would tell them, "Have faith," or "Be calm, sure, confident."

It was during this visit to Bombay that the first steps were taken towards opening a house in Calcutta, which the Daughters of St. Paul were able to do in July, 1956.

Almost immediately after her return to Italy, Mother Thecla set out for the houses of Spain and Portugal.

The book centers of Barcelona and Valencia were functioning well, as also the three agencies for the distribution of films and catechetical shorts.

Vocations were flourishing; some candidates had received the religious habit in March, 1954, the same year that the book center of Valladolid had opened. During Mother Thecla's current visit, the sisters of Spain saw an opportunity to establish themselves in San Fernando de Henares on the outskirts of Madrid; this they did in April, 1956.

The first Pauline sisters had arrived in Portugal in 1950. Shortly after Mother Thecla's visit, they opened their book center in Porto and began to hold very successful "days of the Gospel." They also carried out collective distribution, beginning especially in the hospitals.

The year 1955 had not ended when Mother Thecla began a new journey—her tenth. She stopped first in London, to witness firsthand the beginnings of the Daughters of St. Paul in England. The preceding May, the sisters had taken up residence in Langley, about twelve miles from the British capital, and they had already held their first "feast of the Gospel" for three hundred Italian families. They had also opened a book center.

Then Mother Thecla flew to the United States. In their desire to make themselves "all to all," she and the sisters did not want to leave any possible area of apostolic activity undiscovered, so that the word of God would germinate everywhere. It was during this particular visit that Mother Thecla and the superior in the United States asked permission of the bishop of San Diego, California, to open a new convent in that diocese. Permission was gladly granted. Thus, the house of San Diego came to be called "Mother Thecla's house."

A few months after the opening of the San Diego book and film center, another center would be opened in Buffalo, New York.

Mother Thecla continued on to Canada—destination, Montreal. On the very day after Mother Thecla's arrival, the first issue of the magazine *Voi, Vérité et Vie* was released. Father Alberione had told the sisters, "A magazine fosters unity, generates enthusiasm and gives encouragement. Pay the Divine Master real homage in this year dedicated to Him. Have trust in Him."

Quite worried about this activity of publishing a magazine, since it requires great effort,

the sisters had not concealed their difficulties from
the Founder and Co-foundress, nor from the archbishop, Cardinal Leger.

But Cardinal Leger told them: "Difficulties
do not constitute sufficient grounds for failing to
carry out an apostolic undertaking." Only three
months later the subscriptions numbered in the
thousands.

Shortly after Mother Thecla's arrival in Mexico,
the first Spanish issue of *Via, Veritas et Vita* was
released.

The book centers in Mexico City and Puebla
were doing well. In Bogotá, Colombia, Mother
Thecla had the pleasure of meeting a nice little
group of novices, who had begun their novitiate the
preceding year.

In 1955, the Daughters of St. Paul in Santiago,
Chile, had begun to carry out the technical apostolate. They were printing a catechetical magazine.

Buenos Aires was actively involved in the
radio apostolate. The book centers of Rosario and
Santa Fe were functioning well. The new house
and book center of Tucumàn had also opened at the
beginning of 1955, and the Argentine film apostolate had been begun.

Mother Thecla returned to Italy on Decem-
ber 12. After this long journey, it was necessary for her
to spend a longer period in Rome than usual. After
the exertion of 1955, she spent the first seven months
of 1956 following from the motherhouse the various
Pauline apostolic undertakings being carried on
throughout the world. But nevertheless, at the end
of July, she decided to pay a brief visit to England,
where the investiture of the first Irish aspirants had
been held at the beginning of the year.

MUCH ACTION, MUCH PRAYER

"All of Us Are Missionaries"

Pausing to look at the record of Mother Thecla's tireless activity up to this point, we must say that her accomplishments were prodigious. The Congregation was expanding its apostolate with an accelerated rhythm, setting up typographies and book centers in every continent, producing books and other publications. (Christmas, 1955, saw the beginning of *Così*, a magazine for women, which had a wide distribution in the beginning.)

Mother Thecla's role was extraordinarily demanding; at one and the same time she had to mould the Daughters of St. Paul to carry out the expansion of this great undertaking and also spur on all the apostolic activities.

Since she had uncommon human gifts, to which she joined virtue—acquired through an insistent desire for perfection and the practice of self-control—the formation of the Daughters of St. Paul stemmed from a sure source. During her visits to the convents, whether at home or abroad, she interested herself in every problem, which she prudently studied together with her sisters. She was as concerned about the health of each one as she was about the construction of buildings, as concerned about chapel furnishings as about the latest type of typographical machinery to be acquired.

She was as interested in the printing of a simple leaflet for distribution as she was in the great printings of the Gospel, of the Bible in various languages and local dialects, of liturgical books, of the comprehensive series of catechisms, of the collected teachings of the Popes and Fathers of the Church.

Mother Thecla followed the activity of St. Paul Films and the preparation of filmstrips. She took an interest in the book centers, in the stock of undistributed books in the storerooms, in the various forms of diffusion, whether on an individual or collective basis. She was interested in "book days" and the great "Bible weeks" that she continually encouraged. She concerned herself with book displays in modest parish halls and with vast programs on a national scale. And she also turned her attention to records, when the Paulines launched out into this apostolate.

In the course of her continual travels throughout the world, Mother Thecla had acquired a firsthand knowledge of various peoples of differing races, religions and cultures. Hence, she possessed a great wealth of experience, all of which she imparted to her daughters as they set out for these lands or struggled to insert themselves into their new fields of apostolate. She urged them to appreciate the characteristics of the peoples they were to meet. Above all, she exhorted them to love the people just as they were, accepting everything about their nation that was good and beautiful.

Once she told her sisters, "Adaptation to the characters and temperaments of peoples will exert a great influence. There is a great variety of characters in the world, and to expect to standardize them would be to expect the impossible..,. Together with good qualities, every nationality has defects, and vice-versa; *no one is to be looked down upon.* Let us love, and love always. In love we find the way to do all the good we can."

And she would conclude, "One shows profound wisdom, breadth of vision and great-heartedness in being able to understand all men and help them transform their qualities into virtue!"

Mother Thecla was a missionary to the core. She truly felt called to an ecumenical, universal apostolate.

"We are all missionaries," she would say. "Let us go to the missions with our thoughts, with our intentions, with our prayers, and by carrying out our apostolate well and for the glory of God."

This was why she was able to understand all the worries of bishops, pastors and other priests, who often asked her to send her daughters into their nations and dioceses to set up new centers of apostolate. And when she was able to comply and send her sisters to open new houses, especially in other lands, how great was her joy! Every time she returned from visiting the convents overseas, her eyes revealed her torment at not being able to bring the Gospel message to everyone. She often repeated to her sisters, "Doesn't it pain you to think of so many unbelievers who have not been enlightened by the rays of God's grace? We who were born in Christian lands, of Catholic families, do not understand what good we are doing in bringing a good word to these people."

Another time she said, "All those who do not realize they are idolaters, all who are in good faith, will be saved, because God's mercy is infinite; but we must help them...."

And to back up her statement, she gave what was for her a sure confirmation: "The Founder has this greatly at heart. When he speaks of the Orient, you can see how it pains him. He says, 'Reflect that half the human race lives there. What a pain to see these intelligent people still engulfed in error!' "

After sharing these thoughts with her sisters, she would conclude by urging, "Let us ask God to give us the grace of a universal mentality—a great heart like that of St. Paul for the salvation of many souls, so we may be teachers of all."

A Great Contemplative

But it must not be thought that this intense activity of Mother Thecla harmed her recollection and interior life. As a reliable witness says, "The greatness of this apostolic soul and the fruitfulness of her work had a very important and fundamental source—her profound spirit of prayer. Mother Thecla was such a great apostle and educator of apostles because she was a great contemplative at the same time. She achieved a perfect blend of the most extensive apostolic activity and the most intense union with God.

She was a contemplative in action. Perhaps better than any other, this expression outlines the spiritual personality of Mother Thecla Merlo. Hers were not two separate lives but only one, not action divorced from contemplation, but action that is contemplation and contemplation that is action. Mother Thecla prayed in order to remain united to God and acted in order to love Him, communicate Him and serve Him in her neighbor.

Many are the witnesses to her spirit of prayer. One morning, back when the motherhouse was still in Alba, a sister knocked on the door of Mother Thecla's office. When she entered, she found the mother general in prayer, elbows resting on the work table, hands folded under her chin, gaze fixed on a picture of the Pietà on the wall before her. Her cheeks were wet with tears.

Also once it happened that the sister-photographer had to finish a vocational filmstrip and needed a photograph of the superior general.

"But you are not going to do business with my photos, are you?" Mother Thecla asked jokingly. However, she went to chapel as the sister wished, asking humbly and simply, "How should I pose? What should I do?"

"Mother Thecla, kneel here in the first pew and then pray the way you usually do; pray, too, for the sisters who just left for the missions."

Recalls this sister, "No sooner had I finished speaking than she was already deeply recollected. I peacefully took a dozen photos without her even realizing it."

One Christmas morning Mother Thecla participated in three Masses in the chapel of the general motherhouse, since she was not feeling well and had not gone to the Queen of Apostles Shrine for Mass. Soon thereafter, she came into her office with tears in her eyes.

"Are you crying, Mother Thecla?" the sisters asked.

"I was reflecting on the reading of the third Mass," she replied, "where it says, 'All of them will grow old like a garment....but you are the same, and your years will have no end.' Isn't it a beautiful thought?"

During meetings of the Congregation's general council, the topics discussed were often so difficult that a decision could not be reached. Mother Thecla would utter this or a similar expression: "Oh, how little we are! It would be better for us to go to chapel to pray. Let us go to pray; God will enlighten us." And she would rise and go straight to chapel.

One of the members of the council states, "At first this attitude annoyed me. It seemed an easy way to avoid facing up to the difficulty. But then when I saw the way she would come up with the solution, I understood that she tried to resolve these problems in the light of God."

Often on Sundays, with simplicity, Mother Thecla would address some words to her daughters. The sisters recall what she said to them on a certain Trinity Sunday. These expressions, in particular, struck them:

"We speak of the Blessed Trinity too little. We must honor the Trinity by making the sign of the cross well and saying the 'Glory be' well—but often we do this by force of habit and superficially."

"From that day on," more than one sister declares, "every time I saw her making the sign of the cross, I stopped to reflect. Her own sign of the cross was truly an act of adoration."

In 1957, Mother Thecla had to undergo a major operation. This took place in the Queen of Apostles Hospital, which had been built for the sick sisters in 1949. In this hospital she was to spend her last months; here the final steps in her pilgrimage to perfection would be taken.

Even though the operation was successful, at least two years were to pass before Mother Thecla would be able to resume her intense rhythm of labors

and journeys. Hence in 1958, she sent another sister
to visit her daughters in Manila on the occasion of the
consecration of that city's cathedral.

It was a joy for Mother Thecla to arrange for
other sisters at the motherhouse to come into direct
contact with the Daughters of St. Paul spread throughout the world. Already she had a presentiment that
the course of her life was on the descending swing,
and she wanted to make sure that the unity she had
maintained with her sisters would continue with
others as they gradually assumed more and more
responsibilities in the Congregation. Hence, when
her presence was not required, she sent her closest
collaborator to the United States, saying, "You
know, I thought of sending you because the sisters
will be happy to see you and you will profit from
the visit. One learns much from visiting our communities."

The Eleventh Trip to America

On the morning of August 23, 1956, an automobile with five sisters aboard left Montreal, bound
for Toronto. They arrived there at about 10:30 p.m.
and settled down for the night in a small, five-room
lodging, completely bare. They had to sleep on the
floor that first night, but were happy to perform this
penance in order to found a new center of apostolate.
Accounts of this foundation describe how the little
house was soon furnished with absolute necessities,
while the sisters began almost at once to distribute
their wholesome publications in the homes. They
also carried out that important task already described
—parish census—and visited factories, schools and
offices.

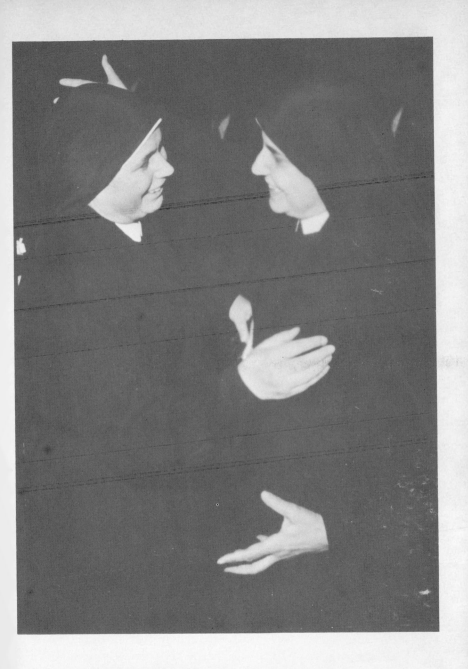

**With her characteristic joy and warm enthusiasm,
Mother Thecla welcomes back to Rome
her Vicar General, returning from the U.S.**

The Shrine of the Queen of Apostles in Rome

Mother Thecla with the Reverend Founder and the major superiors of various countries after the first General Chapter in 1957

**With the Reverend Founder on the
grounds of the Queen of Apostles Hospital for Religious
in Albano, Italy.**

Mother Thecla with her Vicar General, Mother Ignatius.

**With His Eminence, Richard Cardinal Cushing,
at the Boston Novitiate.**

Mother Thecla was a woman of action,
but a woman of contemplation too,
totally immersed in God.

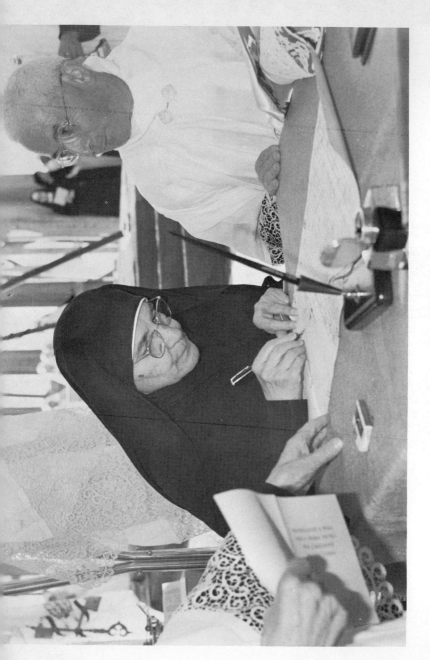

Signing the scroll for the cornerstone of the new church at the Queen of Apostles Hospital, blessed by His Eminence Richard Cardinal Cushing

Paying homage to His Holiness on the occasion of the visit of Pope Paul VI to the Queen of Apostles Hospital.

Picture of Christ in agony contemplated by Mother Thecla in the days of her illness and before her death.

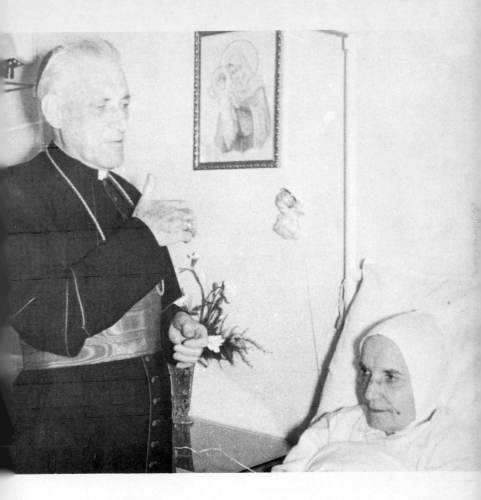

His Eminence, Richard Cardinal Cushing,
blessing Mother Thecla.

Though gravely ill, she could still enjoy the company
of her beloved sisters and also receive distinguished
visitors, as His Excellency, Governor John A. Volpe
of Massachusetts.

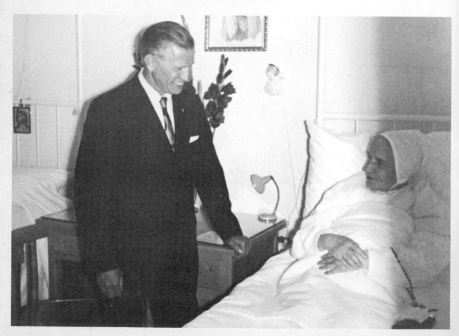

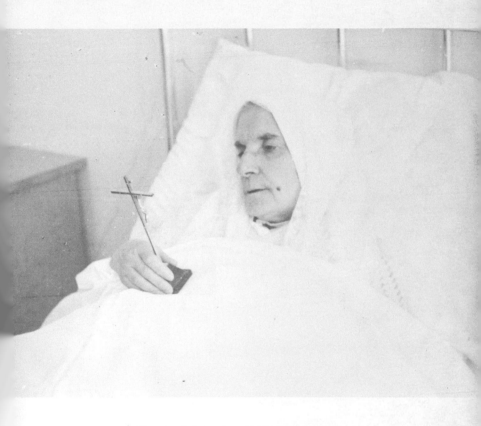

**Thanksgiving after Holy Communion
during her last illness.**

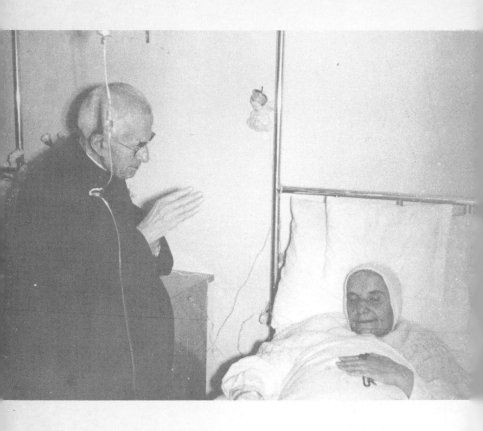

The Reverend Founder, Father Alberione,
blessing Mother Thecla in her last illness.

Members of all the Pauline Congregations and relatives were present for the funeral Mass of Mother Thecla in the Shrine of the Queen of Apostles in Rome.

"The way traced out by Mother Thecla is a broad path,
spacious and glowing, which rises toward
the heights of perfection."

Father Alberione

After the initial difficulties had been overcome, collective distribution proceeded in a manner
that was truly satisfying, especially after the sisters
surmounted financial obstacles and purchased a
second car. They were able to set up their first
school and family libraries. Soon they began to hold
their first book fairs. In 1959, an Italo-Canadian group
that the bishop had established to help them gave
the sisters the means to open the book center.

Mother Thecla made a special stop at Toronto
during her eleventh tour of the houses of America,
which took place after her operation of 1957. She
had arrived in Boston in September, 1959, especially
to visit the house of formation, which had been
transferred there from Derby, New York, and where
the apostolic activities had increased and progressed
greatly. During this visit to the United States, Mother
Thecla gladly gave permission to accept the invitation of the bishop of Miami to open a book center
in his diocese. Then Mother Thecla contacted her
daughters in Toronto.

The press apostolate was strictly necessary
in Canada; however, if the sisters truly wished to
penetrate into every environment, this apostolate
required specific training. It was necessary to know
three languages — French, English and Italian.
Mother Thecla encouraged her sisters in this undertaking.

From Canada, Mother Thecla continued
on to Mexico, where the typography had been
inaugurated in 1956. She wanted a new central
house to be built for the province. This house was
to be completed in March, 1963.

Continuing her tour, in Bogotá Mother Thecla
gave impetus to the subscription campaign for the

magazine *Famiglia Cristiana* in Spanish. She also
endeavored to have new book centers opened,
without losing the chance of having a larger and
more functional house for formation, as well as a
typography.

On this journey, Mother Thecla also visited
Caracas in Venezuela, where the first Daughters
of St. Paul had arrived from Bogotá in May, 1956.

In Chile Mother Thecla visited the new
novitiate house. Great was her joy at the over 10,000
copies of the catechetical magazine *Camino, Verdad
y Vida* that had been produced. In March, 1958,
the first illustrated catechism for the elementary
grades had also been released; thus, the Daughters
of St. Paul of Santiago were ready to respond—at
least in part—to diocesan catechetical needs.

In Buenos Aires, Argentina, Mother Thecla
encouraged the "feasts of the Gospel" and "Bible
weeks" and especially radio transmission over the
station Radio Spendid.

She also visited the sisters of Mendoza, where a
small community had been living since January,
1956. A book center and St. Paul film agency were
also operating in that city.

Mother Thecla also had an opportunity to witness the activity of the sisters of Corrientes; these
had opened their house in August, 1957, setting up
a center of diffusion for books and films soon afterwards.

It was during this visit that Mother Thecla
improved the organization of the book center of
Resistencia, which had been opened in 1958, upon
the bishop's invitation.

During this visit to São Paulo, Brazil, Mother
Thecla marveled at the development of her daughters' apostolate. From March, 1956, they had been

printing the catechist's monthly, *Way, Truth and Life* in Portuguese; and in May, 1958, upon the bishop's invitation they had opened an international center to provide catechetical material for the entire diocese. Mother Thecla also encouraged the Brazilian radio apostolate—which was being carried out in São Paulo, Curitiba and Uruguaiana—and the development of the apostolate of records as catechetical aids.

Returning to Rome, she passed through Portugal, where she visited the houses of Porto and Lisbon.

The Thrust into Africa

Even today one remains astounded when considering the places visited in the course of these journeys and the extraordinary activity of this woman, who never gave herself an instant of respite yet never let herself be suffocated by action. Her activity always bubbled up from an inner wellspring, which was rendered inexhaustible by her continual vigilance and the ascetical discipline she acquired in direct communion with God.

Especially after her operation, when she did not have as much strength as she had had formerly, Mother Thecla was full of new ideas and even more watchful over her sisters. On April 27, 1957, the first general chapter of the Daughters of St. Paul was held, with, of course, the reconfirmation of Mother Thecla as Superior General.

Rome was astir with the great movements that would lead up to the Second Vatican Council. A whole climate of renewal pervaded the various religious congregations, and, as we have seen, Mother Thecla's activity in the Federation of Major

Superiors was greatly appreciated. Together with a profound interior life, she possessed a sense of realism and balance that made her capable of devoting herself to many activities, besides the principal activity of responding to the infinite requests that her daughters showered upon her from all over the world.

Since Mother Thecla had visited her daughters' communities and had given practical advice right on the scene, it was reasonable that her correspondence should grow, making her a participant in everything being done. It was reasonable, too, that the difficulties that arose should also be submitted to her. The amount of correspondence was exhausting, but Mother Thecla nonetheless answered her mail promptly. The sisters affirm that she could detail a solution to the most complicated situation in just a few phrases. This showed a profound intuition and — above all — love.

Among her other activities, Mother Thecla joyfully supported "Ut Unum Sint," a center to promote the reunion of our separated brethren. She made available to the center a sister who was to keep in touch with the bishops, in order to carry out undertakings on the ecumenical level.

This center's usefulness could be seen during the Council, when ecumenical activity was one of the great directives and hopes of the bishops, who were spurred on by Pope John himself. In fact, on December 16, 1960, Pope John approved "Ut Unum Sint" as a primary union. This was like a seal set on this intense activity undertaken for the benefit of the Church.

In September of that year, so as not to lose her constant habit of going to see her sisters, Mother Thecla visited the houses of London and Madrid.

Another project, too, had come to her mind. None of her long travels through the world had ever taken her to Africa. However, she had followed the adventures of her sisters there from 1958, the year they had set out for Leopoldville in the Congo (now Kinshasa, Zaire). Two priests of the Society of St. Paul had prepared the house for them, but the sisters had been especially pressed to come by the Scheuts Fathers, priests of the Congregation of the Immaculate Heart of Mary, who operated a book center in Leopoldville.

Dressed in the white habits worn in Africa, the sisters wanted to begin distributing books among the people, but the Scheuts Fathers would not permit it. "It isn't suitable for white sisters to go about to the houses and villages of the blacks," they said. "You will work in the book center and also in the library of the University Lovanium."

Because the Pauline priests were of the same opinion, the two young sisters obeyed and set to work in the book center, which was called *Croix du Congo*. There they perfected their French and studied Lingala, one of the local dialects.

Nevertheless, as soon as two more sisters arrived, they decided to begin distribution, as they desired. To obtain the necessary permissions, they came to an understanding with the apostolic delegate and the bishop. Then, without the knowledge of the Scheuts Fathers, they began successfully to visit the homes of the Africans. When the Scheuts Fathers became aware of the sisters' extraordinary work and saw the good that was being done, they could not do otherwise than let them continue, but on one condition: they were not to give up the book center.

In January, 1959, with the first uprisings that led to Congolese independence, the book center and other European buildings were burned. Since the priests did not feel inclined to start over from scratch, the Daughters of St. Paul undertook the project instead. On October 9, 1959, they opened a new book center.

In May of the same year, two sisters had left Leopoldville for Elizabethville, now Lubumbashi, where the bishop had invited them to open a house. Certainly, the situation was not the calmest, this being a period of popular uprisings and war, following upon the secession of Katanga from the Belgian Congo. Nonetheless, the sisters continued their apostolic activities until December, 1961, when the civil war constrained them to leave.

It was shortly before the sisters' departure for Elizabethville that Mother Thecla arrived in Leopoldville to see the situation and personally give the sisters her suggestions.

AT THE FINISH LINE
AFTER THE LONG RACE

The First Edition of the Gospel in Chinese

Although the trip to Africa had tired her greatly, Mother Thecla did not grant herself any rest. From that time on, the Founder decreed that a sister should accompany her on her journeys. And this was what happened when she boarded a plane to visit the houses of the Far East in 1962. It was her twelfth long journey.

She stopped in Calcutta, then in Manila.

In the main house of Manila, Mother Thecla became ill and had to stay in bed for a few days. It was decided to summon the older sisters and the superiors of the various houses scattered throughout the Philippines. Thus, they would be able to see and speak with Mother Thecla without making her undergo the fatigue of traveling from one distant island to another.

One day, all of a sudden, Mother Thecla got up and said to her sister companion, "You know, I've had an inspiration. Come to make the visit with me"—and by "visit" she meant the daily hour of adoration that is part of the rule for the Daughters of St. Paul—"then I'll tell you what I thought of."

They went to chapel and prayed for an hour. When they came out Mother Thecla said, "I've decided to visit the sisters in the small convents instead of having only the superiors come here. Send them word. We'll leave tomorrow morning."

The sister had no choice but to agree.

This trip consisted of a series of short flights from island to island. It was tiring. Nevertheless, Mother Thecla was always tranquil and gay, encouraging the sisters, helping them resolve their problems, spurring them on. As always she was the soul of every recreation period.

But at the conclusion of these travels through the Philippines, Mother Thecla again had to be confined to bed. Severe pains in her legs caused her much discomfort, but she did not complain. She was content with this suffering, "for the sanctification of the sisters and the people with whom they come in contact."

In Formosa Mother Thecla visited the two houses of Kaohsiung and Taipei, which the sisters had opened in May, 1959, and June, 1960, respectively. She was very pleased to see the progress they had made in learning Chinese, indispensable for the apostolate. But above all, she rejoiced at the sight of the first Chinese edition of the Gospel.

From Formosa Mother Thecla continued on to Japan, where a new house had been established in Sendai. When the bishop of that city had met the Daughters of St. Paul in Osaka, he had said, "I expect you to come to my diocese as soon as possible. You will work well there as you do here."

The house of Sendai was founded in November, 1957, and the book center in March, 1958.

A house had also been established in Takamatsu in February, 1959, and one in Nagasaki in March, 1960.

In Seoul, Korea, Mother Thecla met the new aspirants. When the first Korean girl had entered the

Congregation in September of the preceding year, Mother Thecla had not imagined what was to happen soon thereafter. In February a fine group of girls asked to enter. Upon meeting them, Mother Thecla accepted five into the aspirancy; the others had to wait "because there wasn't enough room for them."

Before returning to Italy by way of Manila, she also passed through Australia, where in addition to the house of Sydney, that of Adelaide had been opened.

When Mother Thecla returned to Rome in May, 1962, it seemed that she would have to end her continual travels. The sisters of the Orient had seen that she was very tired. They had had the presentiment that this would be their Mother's last journey. Yet, this very same year, Mother Thecla chose to undertake her thirteenth round of visits. This time she set out for the United States, where she took great interest in the sisters' rapidly-developing catechetical apostolate, so dear to the heart of the Founder. The technical apostolate in Boston was flourishing, as was the apostolate of diffusion in all the houses, especially that of New York. The new house of Miami was another link in the chain of book and film centers that stretched from coast to coast: Boston, Mass.; Fitchburg, Mass.; Buffalo, N.Y.; Youngstown, Ohio; Miami, Fla.; Alexandria, La.; San Antonio, Tex.; and San Diego, Calif. Shortly after Mother Thecla's return to Rome, another center would be opened in Bridgeport, Conn.

On this visit to the United States and Canada, Mother Thecla was accompanied by the superior in charge of the houses of the States, who confides that it was precisely during this journey that she came to know Mother Thecla more intimately:

"As I gradually came to know her better, I saw that she truly lived 'the hope of heaven.' Her conversations and letters were filled with expressions that showed this continual aspiration of hers. When I went to speak to her of the difficulties of the great province of the United States, she would listen to me maternally and then conclude, 'The Lord has permitted this for your good. There are difficulties, sufferings and worries; however, you have seen that there are many sufferings in Rome, too.... But one beautiful day it will all be over, and we will find ourselves all united in heaven with the Blessed Trinity, with Mary most holy, with our dear ones and with the sisters who have gone before us. This is our joy and our comfort. Courage!'"

At the Service of the Council Fathers

When Mother Thecla returned from her North American tour, the bishops began to arrive in Rome for the Second Vatican Council, opened by Pope John on October 11, 1962.

Mother Thecla knew many bishops from all the continents; that is, the shepherds of the dioceses where her daughters were carrying out their mission. For one who had made service to the Church through the apostolate of the media of communication the sole ideal of her life, the presence of these shepherds in Rome filled her soul with joy. It can be said that no day passed without some bishop's visiting the general house of the Daughters of St. Paul.

Mother Thecla received them not only with her usual solicitude but also with the open eye of a mother. Some bishops, especially those from developing nations, were in need of much. For many, the

Roman winter was cold. Mother Thecla provided them with woolen clothing, having invited the sisters to give in whatever brand new woolen undershirts they had; when this supply ran out, she did not hesitate to ask some factories for what the poor bishops needed.

She told the sisters, "It is our duty to help them, because they are the shepherds of the churches where our sisters are. They already feel uneasy being so far away from home; they should not have to suffer for other reasons."

Furthermore, she managed to organize a very specific service: every week two sisters would set out by car for the various hotels where the bishops were staying and pick up their personal laundry, which the sisters would then wash, iron and deliver. This was their regular practice for the entire duration of the Council; even when Mother Thecla was no longer with them, the sisters continued to render the service she had wished them to give.

Through the charity she exercised in regard to the Council fathers, Mother Thecla opened up another channel of communication with her sisters. Returning to their dioceses between the annual sessions of the Council, the bishops sought out the Daughters of St. Paul and recounted the favors they had received from Mother Thecla. Thus, the mutual charity between these servants of the Church and their shepherds grew ever stronger.

At the end of 1962, although tired and ailing, Mother Thecla did not want to forego her custom of visiting the houses of Italy; she set out for Sicily and Calabria.

"She was very tired," relates the sister who accompanied her, "but she did not complain. She was always ready to give of herself in order to please others. When asked how she felt, she unfailingly replied with a smile and concluded, 'Everything for heaven, for the good of the Congregation and the good of souls.' She was careful, always concerned about not displeasing her daughters."

"Let Us Lend Our Feet to the Gospel"

"On February 5, 1963," recalls a Daughter of St. Paul, "Mother Thecla made this confidence to me: 'We are not well, you know...but we are not even sick enough to stay in bed, so we must go ahead, even though we are ill and in pain. I feel that things are really not going well, but it will be as the good Lord wants.' In these last months her face was furrowed with fatigue and pain, but she conserved her serenity to the end."

Mother Thecla underscored her presentiment of what was soon to take place by renewing the offering of her life for the Congregation. She also felt a great desire to visit her distant sisters once more.

One day in 1961, she had written to the mistress of novices: "Tomorrow, the feast of the Most Holy Trinity, I want to make an offering of my life, that all the sisters may be saints." And when writing to all the sisters at the end of the same year, she made her decision official, as it were: "I want you all saints; for this I have offered my life."

This declaration only shortly preceded her fourteenth journey, which was to be her last. It was to the Congo.

"What suffering!" she had sometimes exclaimed, when thinking of her sisters engaged in the apostolate in Africa. "Who knows how they are, now that these disturbances are taking place! How can one go to see them?"

At the time of the uprising that had struck the house of the Daughters of St. Paul in Elizabethville, the sisters had described the bombardment, their fear and the necessity of seeking shelter elsewhere. Mother Thecla had wanted to go to them at once, but the sisters would not permit it.

"But," she replied, "what would it matter if I were to suffer, too...aren't they suffering? I want to see them, to know firsthand how they are. Who knows how frightened Sister ... (and she gave the name) must be! Her health is weaker than the others. And who knows how fearful her companion has been. Permit me to go!"

Nonetheless, her physical condition had not allowed this risky journey. But she did go as soon as she could. It was May, 1963.

"My lasting impression of Mother Thecla," recalls the sister who accompanied her, "is her love for God and His glory — that the Gospel be known for the good of souls. The sisters told her of some financial difficulties and their sadness over the books that had been destroyed. Mother Thecla promised books and Gospels, even if the sisters could not pay for them.... 'What counts,' she said, 'is to be able to do good to these souls. Money doesn't count. Do good. Sow the good.'"

This was her characteristic way of doing things. On other occasions, too, in other regions when the difficulties of the apostolate had been great and the probable closing of some house was being faced, she would be quick to intervene: "Oh, no! Let us not close that house. It is in a poor district, in which there is a great need for religious instruction, in which even clergy are scarce. If we don't help them, who will? We are here for this."

And also when she returned from her travels in the Orient, especially in India, she was completely absorbed in this preoccupation: "What teeming cities! Streets swarming with people.... Millions and millions of people who do not know God.... Oh, if only there were many of us, to bring the Gospel to everyone!"

To the sisters in Japan she wrote: "Now you are in your field of apostolate. Thanks be to God! Right in the missions, among the unbelievers. What a grace! As soon as you can, begin to say some good words here and there, to bring light into that darkness. Every day at Mass and during the Visit to the Blessed Sacrament, I recommend to God the unbelievers of China, Japan and the entire world."

And she continued: "The Founder is preoccupied; he says that the Gospel spreads little. Pray much about this. Let us lend our feet to the Gospel—that it may run and extend itself."

Now, however, Mother Thecla's course was almost run.

The Council Approves the Decree on Social Communications

Mother Thecla arrived in Rome—upon her return from the Congo—when all Christendom was praying for the ailing Pope John XXIII. She herself had seen him for the last time at Castelgandolfo on September 3, 1960, and had written to the sisters: "Yesterday I went to an audience with the Holy Father at Castelgandolfo, not by myself, but with a few other people. We kissed his hand and asked his blessing for everyone. I'm so happy."

When Pope John died, on June 3, 1963, she replied thus to a letter from the sisters of the United States: "Here, too, they say that Pope John is a saint. We expect to receive many graces from our deceased Holy Father. You should have seen the procession to his tomb—flowers everywhere and everyone praying. Now let us pray for whomever will be elected."

A few weeks after his election, the new Pope, Paul VI, visited the sisters' Queen of Apostles Hospital, in Albano, where Mother Thecla was convalescing from the illness that had seized her (in June she had suffered from her first cerebral spasm). On the eve of the Pope's arrival she herself gave the news: "Tomorrow morning we will have the grace of a Mass celebrated here by the Holy Father."

One can imagine her joy in welcoming the Pope to this hospital in which she was staying, the hospital she had wanted to have at the cost of considerable sacrifice.

Before the year's end Mother Thecla tasted another joy—that of holding in her hands the conciliar decree on the media of social communication, *Inter mirifica*, approved by the Council on December fourth. With this decree, the Church recognized "that these media, if properly used, can be of great service to mankind," because "they greatly contribute to men's entertainment and instruction as well as to the spread and support of the kingdom of God"; and the Church exhorted "all men of good will, especially those who have charge of these media, to strive to turn them solely to the good of society, whose fate depends more and more on their proper use. Thus, as was the case with ancient works

of art, the name of the Lord may be glorified by these
new discoveries in accordance with those words of
the Apostle: 'Jesus Christ, yesterday and today, and
the same forever.'"

Notwithstanding her weakness, Mother Thecla
managed to read the decree, and she rejoiced greatly
in it. The promulgation of this conciliar document was
a recognition of the specific mission of the Daughters of St. Paul in the universal Church, and confirmed, with the chrism of magisterial authority, an
ideal and apostolate for which Mother Thecla had
offered her entire life.

The Way of the Cross Before the End

As we have said, Mother Thecla's first bout
with her fatal illness took place in mid-June, 1963.
From that point on, we follow the notes of the sister-
nurse who was nearer to her than anyone else during
the period of her illness.

On the morning of June 16, Mother Thecla
showed that she did not feel well; nonetheless, she
did not want to change the day's program of work. She
talked to the novices, who were on their way to make
their annual retreat at Ariccia, and presided over a
meeting of the general council concerning the
novices' admission to religious profession. During
this meeting, however, the sisters of the council saw
that Mother Thecla was not well. They soon perceived that speaking was an effort for her, as if her
tongue were swollen, and that she often said words
that were not really exact in their context. They began
to worry.

It was the beginning of a cerebral spasm with
the danger of thrombosis. That evening — around

ten o'clock—the malady manifested itself in all its gravity. Hence, it was decided to administer the Sacrament of the Sick.

During the preparations for the anointing, Mother Thecla's body seemed to contract, and she lost consciousness. Her face paled, and her breathing took on a rattling sound. It seemed that the sickness was escalating and that, humanly speaking, nothing more could be done; but toward 3:00 AM, contrary to any expectation, her condition improved slightly. At 5:00 AM, Mother Thecla opened her eyes and asked the sister near her, "What are you doing here?"

"How deeply moved I was," says the sister, "to hear that voice again after such a grave attack!"

A few days later, the crisis could be considered past, but Mother Thecla had been greatly weakened and was unable to resume her usual activities. Her way of the cross had begun. Accustomed to being very active, she made her compulsory inactivity a springboard for more intense union with God. She showed no impatience; rather, she was docile to the doctors, nurses and schedule. She knew how to see God's will in all this, and she prayed—prayed much.

When she could, she went to visit the sisters who were most seriously ill. She followed with interest the early stages in the construction of a new chapel and other additions to the hospital.

From the veranda of her room she could view all the work of construction. One evening, as she stood facing the wing that was being erected, she said to the sister-nurse, "Let's go to sprinkle a little holy water on that wall." And while the superior of the clinic sprinkled some drops of holy water, Mother Thecla began to sing the antiphon of the Asperges, with a voice as warm as ever, even though less robust.

This sprinkling was a practice to which she had always been faithful; it has become traditional among the Daughters of St. Paul.

Writes the same sister: "During August and September, she spent some hours in Rome. But on November 22, her brief trips between Rome and Albano were interrupted by a new cerebral spasm."

This attack marked the most sorrowful station on her way of the cross, for it removed her power of speech, and consequently she was no longer able to communicate any thought. Not only that, but she also found that when she took up her pen, her arm could no longer carry out her commands.

She quickly hid the paper on which she had tried to write something. Then, realizing that she could neither speak nor write, she cried, but it was only an instant of distress. She took hold of herself at once, seeing God's will in this and recalling the offering of her life that she had made for all her daughters in 1961.

On November 29, the novena to the Immaculate Conception began. Around the third day of the novena, Mother Thecla recovered slightly and managed to recite the Hail Mary. She was so happy that tears came to her eyes. She wanted to go to chapel; however, the sisters could not let her. But one day after lunch, with determination and energy she indicated that she wanted to get up. "Let's go!" she said, turning her gaze towards the chapel.

"It was impossible to resist," comments the sister, "so evident was her eagerness to encounter the Eucharistic Master at least for a moment."

Very slowly and with great effort, she reached the chapel. Her eyes fixed themselves on the tabernacle. After remaining in her customary intense recollection for a few minutes, she obeyed the voice of the nurse urging her to leave, and emerged from the chapel satisfied.

Thus she had won a right; every day after lunch she made a brief visit to the Eucharistic Jesus. It was the one walk of the day—down five yards of hallway.

In January, 1964, Mother Thecla was taken into the new wing of the hospital; she would remain there only briefly.

"Heaven Is Conquered with Patience"

What Mother Thecla had written on various occasions was actualized and emphasized during the last weeks of her life:

"When Jesus comes to us, may He always find our hearts full of charity and love, capable of loving others as He has loved us."

"Our whole life must be spent for God."

"All except holiness is nothing."

"Everything passes but heaven."

Mother Thecla had returned from her last journey to the Far East and her last trip to the Congo with sentiments of joy regarding the development of the Congregation, but also with great sorrow, considering the tremendous needs of the Church and the impossibility of reaching everyone. The letters she wrote from those lands constituted a marvelous testimony. More than once, irreligion and paganism filled her eyes with tears, but her faith never wavered.

Now, during her painful illness, she kept the needs of all her sisters more than ever before her. Thus, she awaited God's call with the readiness of one

who believes in His almighty power, with the serene
constancy of one who feels she has done everything she can to accomplish her mission well, and
with joy at being able to give something of herself, her own suffering, for all the souls entrusted
to her and to her daughters.

Death would be an encounter with the Father.
To the chaplain she confided, "How wonderful it
will be to meet the Father! Up there we will be
home!"

She had spoken of this often, even when returning from her journeys, tired and laden with preoccupations. "How many things become easier if we
think of them and view them in the light of heaven!"
she would say. "That beautiful heaven! There we will
see and enjoy God forever. May everything else seem
small to us."

To some of the sick whom she had visited when
she could still walk, she would say, "We will rest in
heaven—isn't it so? There you will not suffer any-
more. There we will enjoy God."

Now, God was calling her.

To another sick sister she said, "Heaven is conquered with patience. Patience is purchased at the
tabernacle."

In a conversation with the sisters, she exhorted,
"Live with the thought of God. We must expect everything from Him and His goodness. Always look up—
to heaven; that is our true homeland. The place the
Divine Master has prepared for us is there. We must
aspire to it; we must arrive there at any cost. And
not just any place at all, but we must aim high, at our
own place."

Mother Thecla had given all to reach the place
God had assigned to her.

"I will never sufficiently appreciate the privilege of having been with Mother Thecla during her last illness," relates the chaplain. "What treasures and riches of grace in that soul! She gave her time of illness the greatest value. Making herself a penitent disciple, she stood out as a teacher of penance, for she used the means of penance that the Church places at our disposal."

When recovering from her first attack, Mother Thecla spoke of the Anointing of the Sick, which she knew she had received a few days before while unconscious. Sincerely and simply, she confessed, "I am aware of more grace within me, and more inspirations. I feel a greater impulse to do good and to cling to the will of God. This I owe to this sacrament."

Recalls the chaplain, "She wanted to receive absolution every day. Almost every evening I paid her a visit. We would hold a brief conversation, followed by absolution. She would say, 'And now, give me absolution; purify me. I have a great need to make up for the past, to prepare myself for my meeting with Jesus. At that encounter I don't want His eyes to find anything in my heart that could displease Him.'"

After her second attack Mother Thecla received a visit from her brother, Father Costanzo, a pastor in Barolo, Piedmont.

A month before, he had written her: "I derive my greeting from the liturgy of these days: *The Lord is near.* St. Paul says: *Rejoice, because the Lord is near*, so that we may receive Him with tranquillity and joy in full resignation to His will."

Because his parishioners knew Mother Thecla, Father Costanzo told them about this meeting with her. "She sat in an arm chair," he said. "The tears that fell from her eyes, jeweling a spontaneous smile, and the hand raised towards heaven, because she could no longer speak, attested to her complete resignation."

On this same occasion, Father Costanzo read aloud the letter that Mother Thecla had sent him for the twenty-fifth anniversary of his ordination.

These are some of its outstanding phrases: "I am very grateful to you. At least once, let me tell you this and thank you. It is because of you that I'm a Daughter of St. Paul. Do you remember that it was you who introduced me to the Theologian? I am most content with my vocation. I wish I had had a thousand lives to dedicate to this noble apostolate, even though there were many troubles and difficulties.

"Remember your sister on this beautiful day; tell the Lord to forgive my lack of correspondence to His graces and to grant that we may all be united in heaven."

The Last Embrace Before the Separation

In its inexorable progress, the illness made its way to the vital centers, closing and destroying the last paths to the fonts of life. In a terrible manner it destroyed that body already consumed.

Of Mother Thecla's last day, a Daughter of St. Paul wrote: "On February 4, we came to Albano to consult together about some matters. Before beginning, we went to see Mother Thecla. It made such an impression on me to see her body so emaciated and her eyes so luminous. She seemed to have the expression and gaze of an innocent child. It was a detached and transparent gaze, in which there were no more human thoughts and preoccupations. She kept on looking at us and smiling. When we entered her room it seemed as if she had been expecting us.

"We said to her, 'Mother Thecla, we have come here to work. Pray for us.'

"'Yes,' she replied. And she smiled—smiled continually.

"When our work had been completed, or rather, at lunch time, Sister Costantina, the superior of the hospital, told us, 'Mother Thecla has already had lunch. She is waiting to greet you before she goes to rest.'

"We returned to her room. There she was, absorbed in contemplating. But, I repeat, I was struck by her gaze—a gaze absorbed and extraordinarily joyous—and the smile of one no longer concerned at all with matters of this world. I said to myself, 'What an expression Mother Thecla has today!' It was almost a premonition, for the next day, at the same hour, Mother Thecla entered her agony."

Early in the morning of February 5, Mother Thecla had the comfort of a visit from the Founder.

The morning passed in suffering, but always she had that same smile, which was no longer of this earth.

The sister-nurse who stayed at Mother Thecla's side until the end relates that around 11:00 AM Mother Ignatius, the vicar general, who was to return to Rome to greet the provincial superior arriving from Spain, stopped in to say good-bye.

"I'm going to Rome, Mother Thecla," Mother Ignatius informed her. "But I'll be back right away."

Mother Thecla gazed at Mother Ignatius long and intently. "Good," she said, smiling.

The vicar general turned to leave. But immediately the nurse called her back, because by a crook of her finger Mother Thecla had indicated a desire for Mother Ignatius to return.

The vicar general drew near the bed and leaned over. Without saying a word, Mother Thecla reached up, embraced her and kissed her. Again she gazed at Mother Ignatius long and intently.

Deeply moved, Mother Ignatius then left the room and went to see a sister who had just had an operation. Not long after this, came the urgent summons: "Mother Thecla is worse."

The vicar general hastened back to the sickroom and noted the sudden aggravation of the patient's condition. Mother Thecla was in agony. That kiss and embrace for Mother Ignatius had been her last good-bye.

"I cannot forget that farewell," declares the superior of the hospital, who had been present at the scene. "I can't forget the last embrace Mother Thecla gave the vicar general before entering her agony. That farewell and embrace seemed to be a sign of the transmission of a heritage — the Congregation."

The sister-nurse relates that Mother Thecla's agony began around 12:30: "We gathered around her to pray. Her face could be described as the face of the dying Christ. Indeed, above her bed hung a picture of Christ in agony that had been painted for her by one of the sister-patients. As she lay there, with her head tilted the same way as that of the Christ above, the same spasmodic expression agonized on her face. The death rattle was first insistent, then stronger and slower.

"I thought to myself, 'How she is suffering! But this is not *her* death. She is dying for someone else, for all of us.'

"The Founder—the person hardest hit by the sorrow—said to us, 'Read the passage of the Gospel that narrates the passion of Christ.'"

Sister Mary Teresa, Mother Thecla's niece, opened the Gospel and began to read. She read as far as the words: "He bowed his head, and delivered over his spirit" (Jn. 19:30).

Father Alberione turned. "Enough," he said. "Now say the formula of profession—loudly."

The agony continued, in soul-rending spasms. The Founder drew as near to her as he could and suggested, "Mother Thecla, offer your life for the Congregation. Offer your life and all your sufferings, that all the members will be saints." Then he stopped and withdrew, too choked up to continue.

Approaching again, the Founder prayed, "Jesus, I believe in You, I hope in You, I love You with all my heart...." Silence fell about the bed, which had become an altar on which a person rich in faith and love was immolating herself.

The rattle became increasingly long, interspersed with moments of silence. At length Mother Thecla opened her eyes, closed them again and relaxed her fingers. The rattle ceased without a tremor.

"She had suffered before," reflects the sister-nurse. "The last instant was most peaceful."

MANY INSTITUTES—ONLY ONE MOTHER

The Sister Disciples of the Divine Master

Mourning about the deathbed of Mother Thecla were not only the Daughters of St. Paul, but also the members of other Pauline institutes.

Mother Thecla's particular relationship with Father Alberione had made her his active cooperator in the foundation and consolidation of the various congregations composing the great Pauline Family. Under the impulse of the Founder's charism, these congregations were linked together in multiple vocations, all directed to the same objective of communicating the word of God.

For example, right at the beginning Mother Thecla had been able to see firsthand that many girls desired in a special way—and as an authentic vocation—to help the new mission in a more distinctly contemplative, rather than actively apostolic, manner. This was a confirmation, on the real-life level, of a desire Father Alberione had already expressed in 1908.

"In 1908," he wrote, "I began to pray and ask others to pray that a religious family would be born which would be dedicated to a hidden life, and consecrated to a triple apostolate—eucharistic, liturgical and priestly—thus to be a wellspring of grace that would flow out upon the other congregations specifically dedicated to the apostolic life." This congregation that the Founder hoped for would be the Sister Disciples of the Divine Master.

In 1924, Father Alberione chose from among the Daughters of St. Paul eight young women destined to form the first nucleus of the new congregation. He separated them from the others. After having given them the name referred to above, he also established a rule of their own. It was February 10, 1924, the feast of St. Scholastica. And Sister Mary Scholastica Rivata was the first superior.

In those early days the Sister Disciples went back and forth between the kitchen and the refectory, the shoe shop and the sewing room, the laundry and the room where Church goods were made. But above all their place was in church. Even at that time was evidenced what was to be a distinctive characteristic of their vocation—adoration of the Eucharistic Christ and a liturgical apostolate.

Mother Thecla constantly endeavored to aid this fruitful branch of the Pauline Family. She knew the thought of Father Alberione, according to which the Sister Disciples were to be like the hidden root of both the Society of St. Paul and the Daughters of St. Paul—"Because," declared Father Alberione, "the source of nourishment for all is the Eucharistic Master, Way, Truth and Life." Also, the Founder explained, "There must be a group of souls who pray and, if need be, immolate themselves, so that the apostolic undertakings will be fruitful."

On March 25, 1924, the first Sister Disciples donned their religious habit. But juridically they remained part of the Daughters of St. Paul as long as Father Alberione felt that it was not yet time to set them apart—also legally—as an independent congregation with its own specific purpose. However, when he did request the ecclesiastical authorities to realize his plan, around 1946, he found himself confronted with unforeseen difficulties.

A situation arose that caused anxiety and suffering, also because some people, although reliable, lacked precise awareness of the Founder's projects.

In this circumstance the virtue and capacity for balance and mediation of the Servant of God, Father Timothy Giaccardo, faithful collaborator of the Founder, and the wisdom and goodness of Mother Thecla shone in a particular way. Mother Thecla remained strong and serene, infusing peace and security, giving a witness of supernatural faith and abandonment in God which she succeeded in communicating to others.

When an ecclesiastical decree, issued August 24, 1946, directed the fusion of the Daughters of St. Paul and Sister Disciples, Mother Thecla immediately drew inspiration from what Father Alberione had written to the Sister Disciples: "Nothing is more sweet, more sure, more meritorious than obedience—and this time great obedience is involved! I am pleased to have you know that the mother general and I are the first to carry out this obedience."

We have precious testimony from Father Giaccardo about Mother Thecla's attitude toward the Sister Disciples who had to merge with the Daughters of St. Paul. Writing to them on October 7 of the same year, he said, "The mother general welcomes all of you, one by one, with a motherly heart. She will have you feel the warmth of the nest and a mother's affection."

Members of the Sister Disciples affirm that Mother Thecla's activity at this time was silent, in-

dustrious and farsighted. Often they saw the effects
of her intervention and action—which were discrete
but fruitful—as she followed her desire to render less
unpleasant the hospitality not wanted by the Sister
Disciples and not easy for the Daughters of St. Paul.

Moreover, although greatly occupied with her
own sisters, Mother Thecla found the time to converse privately with the Sister Disciples. One of
these recalls, "I approached her with a modest list of
things to say and ask about. In a few minutes everything was finished, for only to look at her, so strong
and serene, only to listen to her words of faith, made
the difficulties vanish before they had been set forth.
I came away enlightened, trusting, certain that the
Lord would provide. I understood the strength that
stemmed from her faith and her prayer—almost a
power that communicated the presence of God."

Because of the generous acceptance of the
will of God on the part of Father Alberione and Father
Giaccardo, and because of the daily solicitude of
Mother Thecla, this trial was overcome well—so
well that on March 25, 1947, the Most Reverend
Luigi Grassi, Bishop of Alba, with the consent of
the Holy See, gave diocesan approval to the Sister
Disciples, who thus became independent from the
Daughters of St. Paul. On the following April 3,
Holy Thursday, Father Giaccardo addressed these
words to them in the name of the Founder: "On the
eve of His passion, in His measureless and limitless
love, the Divine Master instituted the Holy Eucharist and the priesthood. On this priestly day and with
the same love He brings you a new juridical life,
full and unique, and calls you to render to His priesthood contributions of prayer and apostolate according to your vocation."

After the new Congregation had also received papal approval (in January, 1948), and its distinction from the Daughters of St. Paul had been conclusively sanctioned, the Sister Disciples were decisively inserted into their specific mission of eucharistic adoration, domestic service in the Pauline houses, and liturgical apostolate. Roles were distinguished, a definitive division of the members was made, and the activities of the Daughters of St. Paul and Sister Disciples were spelled out, as the new statutes required.

During this stage, too, the capability and balance of Mother Thecla could be clearly seen. In fact, she had to devote herself to a ceaseless task of persuading, clarifying, giving advice, maintaining calm, indicating the course to take. On this occasion as well, she repeated a phrase that was habitual with her: "Let us do God's will and let us do it gladly. Everything will straighten out." And she continued, "The two sister Congregations will be strong; they will progress."

Of course, even in the future, those in charge of the Sister Disciples often turned to Mother Thecla to ask her advice, and she counseled them with great sincerity and love, pleased with the progress they were making. "I am happy, really happy for you. The Lord is blessing you; go ahead." And she would speak with them of the Eucharist, the priesthood and the liturgy, in order to emphasize and confirm their vocation.

In 1946, there were already 270 professed Sister Disciples, but with their novices and aspirants in various parts of the world they totaled 400. Mother Thecla was concerned about them, too, during her travels. And in whatever way she could, she recommended them to the Daughters of St. Paul. To her daughters in the United States, she wrote, "I am pleased that you help them; thus, they will go ahead well. If one of you needs to stay with them to help them to start out, do so willingly. I am sure you will go ahead together well."

Very often, when she wrote to the houses of America, Australia and other lands, she sent greetings to the Sister Disciples. And when she sent meditation leaflets or sermons given by the Founder during retreats, she sometimes included a copy for the Sister Disciples, too—especially if they lived near the Daughters of St. Paul—so they could enjoy the same spiritual nourishment.

The "Sisters of Jesus the Good Shepherd"

Mother Thecla lavished the same care on the Sisters of Jesus the Good Shepherd, another Pauline Congregation. Father Alberione chose the first "Pastorelle"—as they soon came to be called—from among the Daughters of St. Paul. It was as if he cut a tender twig from the sturdy trunk of the Institute, that it might grow in other soil. Mother Thecla knew the desires of the Founder, who for years had repeated that pastors and bishops were left alone in their pastoral ministry. As a young priest he himself had helped the pastors of Alba. He knew well the situations in parishes, often deprived of the most ordinary help to prepare people for the sacraments, to give religious instruction, to care for the churches—in short, to carry out all the pastoral activities proper to the miniature Church that is the parish community.

It was precisely in the early years of his priestly ministry that Father Alberione conceived the idea of a religious congregation that would act as a small quantity of leaven inserted into the parish to transform it with Christian life and virtue. But the road the Lord had him travel was quite different. He first had to give strong roots to the plants of the Society of St. Paul and the Daughters of St. Paul, so that the word of God would be spread in the world through the media of social communication. When everything had been straightened out almost completely, his great aspirations could begin to be realized. But he needed the full cooperation of Mother Thecla, who willingly complied with the Founder's desire. To someone else the removal from the Congregation of two sisters (for there were two of them in the beginning) would have seemed an injustice. But Mother Thecla was not one to jealously cling to accumulated treasures; on the contrary, she always viewed with joy the opportunities that presented themselves for the maturation of her sisters' good qualities. She had a very important role in the "baptism" of the newborn congregation.

The first two novices of the "Pastorelle" made their religious profession in February, 1939, and the Congregation soon began to bear good fruit. After a few years Father Alberione declared, "I have come upon the Sisters of Jesus the Good Shepherd conducting model kindergartens, teaching and directing church choirs, training altar boys, making altar breads, laundering and mending altar linens. I have seen them directing sewing classes, giving talks to Catholic youth groups, preparing the sick for the sacraments, helping boys and girls participate in the liturgy, cleaning and decorating churches and altars and making arrangements for marriages to be rectified. I have seen them encouraging the indifferent to make their Easter duty, to join Christian social movements, to attend Sunday Mass. I have seen them distributing food, clothing and help to the poor; guiding children to prepare little dramatic productions; giving religious instructions; preparing children for First Communion and Confirmation; and keeping cemeteries clean and decorous. I have seen them kneeling before the Eucharistic Jesus, making a daily hour of adoration for their own sanctification, for the parish and for pastors of souls."

This description eloquently speaks of growth in activity and spirituality. It is much more eloquent when one reflects that the life of the infant Congregation was taking shape in a period which, by human standards, at least, was quite unfavorable. It really seemed as if the times of the foundation of the Society of St. Paul were being repeated. As then World War I was beginning, so now the new sisters were taking their first steps at the opening of the second global conflict. Nevertheless, these external difficulties did not lessen their effort.

For the first months Mother Thecla gave the "Pastorelle" hospitality. Inspired by a genuine spiritual maternity, she wisely undertook the task of advising them, forming them and at the same time respecting their particular vocation, as the Founder desired.

After the sisters had moved into their first house—in Genzano, near Rome—Mother Thecla went to visit them often, helping them in their difficulties and giving them encouragement. She sustained and guided them when they opened their house of apostolate in San Marzano, Taranto, in October, 1939, and a second in Mass Martana, Perugia, in 1940.

Before any of the "Pastorelle" had earned diplomas, she sent them some Daughters of St. Paul

who were trained teachers. These remained with the
"Pastorelle" until the latter were able to fend for
themselves.

She also helped them materially, especially
during the war. At that time the Daughters of St. Paul
had a small studio of sacred art. Not being able to go
out to distribute books, they made crucifixes, statues
of the Blessed Virgin and other small, sacred objects.
One day Mother Thecla told the sisters to send
some moulds to the "Pastorelle," too, and to teach
them the steps in making these religious articles,
"in order to support themselves in this difficult
period."

Between her two journeys of 1953 — one to the
Far East and one to the Americas — Mother Thecla
was able to share the joy of all the Sisters of Jesus
the Good Shepherd over their Congregation's diocesan approval, granted by the bishop of Albano. At that
time the congregation numbered 200 members. It
had thirty houses in seventeen Italian dioceses and
two in Brazil.

The sister who used to drive Mother Thecla
recalls that the mother general would often say,
"Bring the car. We are going to Genzano. Let's go see
those daughters!"

Many of the "Pastorelle" affirm that Mother
Thecla never tired of hearing of their necessities,
difficulties and even material needs. She would
converse with them as with each of her own sisters.
Whenever she saw that the sisters were somewhat
low in spirits, she would say to her companion,
"You return home. I'll stay here with them."

The same sister relates that in these circumstances Mother Thecla would not show that she had
noticed anything, although she had sensed that
something was not quite right. Since she wanted that

community to be unclouded by shadows, she would improvise a joyous evening of songs, stories and recollections of her travels. Then she would reassure the sisters with reflections drawn from her own life experiences—reflections on faith, love of God, trust in divine Providence.

When Mother Thecla departed, the "Pastorelle" would feel as though they had taken a strong tonic.

The Other Pauline Institutes

Many years later, in 1958, although heavily burdened with the responsibility of her Congregation, Mother Thecla also gave her generous collaboration to other achievements of the Founder. 1958 was the year in which various Pauline institutes were born.

In Rome Father Alberione personally started the "Queen of Apostles" institute for the recruitment of vocations; these sisters were called "Apostoline." They had already been established at Castelgandolfo in 1957, but only on June 29, 1958, did the first sisters—all from Rome—make their religious investiture, followed the next year by profession. In 1959, four of these sisters established themselves in Turin.

Father Alberione sketched the purpose of the institute in a few words: "That all Catholics, with all their energies, with every means, may work for all vocations, for all apostolates."

The activity of the Queen of Apostles Sisters, therefore, was directed primarily to the orientation of youth in the choice of their future and the sensitizing of various environments to the vocational problem, using both traditional and modern means (press, records, films, radio, television, exhibits, etc.). To this end the young sisters began to organize encounters; retreats; courses of spiritual exercises and orientation; vocational "weeks," exhibits, and conventions—in schools, parishes and dioceses.

In 1958, they launched a ten-lesson correspondence course "of life-orientation," which was much appreciated because of its intelligent and modern tone. Two years later the Queen of Apostles Sisters inaugurated a magazine of orientation, *Se Vuoi*, which to this day remains the most complete vocational magazine in Italy.

One can imagine the joy and interest with which Mother Thecla followed the beginnings of this institute, which responded, as has been said more than once, to one of her own great desires — that many vocations would be raised up to spread the word of God everywhere. Because of this, she was a very great help to the Founder, and she herself regarded the "Apostoline" as if they were members of her own family, helping them in their first steps according to their needs.

In that same year, 1958, four secular institutes were approved: the Institute of "Jesus the Priest," for diocesan clergy; the Institute of "St. Gabriel the Archangel," for young laymen; the Institute of "the Blessed Virgin of the Annunciation," for young women; and the Institute of "the Holy Family," for married couples.

These institutes gathered and continue to gather members in the most diverse cities and continents to which the Pauline Family has spread. These are persons who have understood the charism of Father Alberione and want to collaborate with this new form of apostolate while remaining in the world, without a particular habit and without being bound to common life. They—I am speaking above all of the laity—were to carry out the apostolate in the midst of all categories of people. With regard to the priests, the institute planned for them by Father Alberione was the realization of what Pope John XXIII had recommended, stimulating priests to follow the commitment of the religious life in order to better elevate and strengthen their priesthood.

Many members of these institutes recall the benefits they received from Mother Thecla. This is especially true of priests, but also of the fathers of families, professional people, workmen and housewives. Many are the episodes that confirm Mother Thecla's maternal care for them. And she herself, in speaking of these institutes, used to say, "We are all one family. We all have the same Father. Let us all love one another."

Mother Thecla's greatness of soul may be seen from this continual help she rendered to the many undertakings that sprang forth from the extraordinary charism of Father Alberione. She performed a hidden and silent mission, taking a personal interest in everyone. She never stood out, but sustained everything, in a true service of Mary-like presence, of obscurity and sacrifice.

THE INTERIOR "CELL"
OF THECLA MERLO

The Word "On Paper"

It was 1950. In a meditation for the representatives of various orders and congregations attending the first congress of religious, Father Alberione uttered some words that made history.

"There must be the persuasion," he emphasized, "that in these new apostolates, with the new media of social communication, a greater spirit of sacrifice and a more profound piety are required, for these apostolates involve fruitless endeavors, sacrifices of sleep and time, insufficient funds, misunderstandings on the part of many, spiritual dangers of all sorts, discernment in the choice of means....

"Let us save, but first of all, let us save ourselves! We need saints to precede us on these roads as yet untrodden, and in part not even marked out. This is not a matter for amateurs," he noted with emphasis, "but for true apostles."

Then he invited the assembly to consider the status of Christian preaching—its insufficient capacity to penetrate the contemporary world, which instead listens daily to radio, films and television—the new, modern pulpits: "In many regions the priest preaches to a small, vanishing flock in an almost empty church."

And he ended by repeating the words of a great cardinal, Elia Dalla Costa: "Either we look with courage at the reality that lies beyond the little world around us — and then we will see the urgency of a radical transformation of mentality and method — or else in the space of a few years we shall have created a wasteland around the Master of life, and life will justly eliminate us as dry, useless, cumbersome branches."

Everyone can judge the sharp-sightedness of this declaration which by-passed the incidental, and pointed decisively to the developments that mankind's new horizons imposed on the choice and updating of the presentation of the word of God.

The Word of God is the incarnate Word who made Himself the Master (Teacher) of humanity. Preaching about this Word cannot be restricted as to the means with which it is done; oral and written preaching are both authentic. The proclamation does not make distinction between means, nor does it discriminate as to instruments. Hence, Father Alberione did not hesitate to adopt an expression of Bishop Montini, now Paul VI, who declared when speaking to writers: "You take the word of God and reclothe it in ink, type and paper and send it into the world so dressed. It is God's word clothed this way — God 'on paper.' You give God on paper (in Italian, *incartato*), as Mary gave men God incarnate (*incarnato*). *Incartato* and *incarnato* correspond."

It was an audacious and almost irreverent parallel, but how true! To be teachers of God's word with all means is in essence the Pauline Family's reason for being. In the course of the sixty years of its history this family of institutes has penetrated into the unfathomable riches of Jesus the Master, Way, Truth and Life, radiating these internally among the members and externally towards the whole world. The result has been interior and apostolic universalism.

Interior universalism can be measured by the drive for complete human, doctrinal, spiritual and ascetical formation. The very multiplicity within the Pauline Family, with one institute rising up after another, each for a specific purpose, testifies to the universalism of this spirituality within the members. But this universalism is to be apostolic. "Every apostolate and good undertaking must be illuminated and sustained. One must bring Christ," Father Alberione exhorted, "into the hearts of all peoples. One must make the Church's presence felt in connection with every problem, in a spirit of adaptation and comprehension for all necessities both social and individual."

This universalism, assimilated through the diligent meditation of the Apostle of the Gentiles, (the Founder said: "We wanted a saint excelling in holiness who was at the same time an example of apostolate, and St. Paul united both sanctity and apostolate in himself)—this universalism Father Alberione planted in his sons and daughters. He told them, "With regard to the world, you are the city placed on the mountain top.... In the first place you must give the doctrine that saves; in the second place you must permeate all human thought and knowledge with the Gospel. Do not speak only of religion, but speak of everything in a Christian manner."

After the Founder, Thecla Merlo was the most consistent and faithful personification of this idea. We have followed her eventful and active life in every step, emphasizing, however, that her activity did not detract from recollection and prayer. Yet her complete personality could not be grasped without entering into the secret recesses of her soul. The adventure of Father Alberione was already in itself a fascination for someone who thirsted to preach the Gospel as she did, but the appeal of apostolic action could not suffice; this action had to be sustained by a profound spirituality, which would enable her to overcome enormous difficulties and satiate her immense hunger for God.

The "Mother" of the Paulines

In the program launched by Father Alberione there was a whole new way of living the Gospel and presenting it to the world of today. Of living it: Father Alberione decisively removed the demarcation between action and contemplation, bringing the sacred back into profane activity and ennobling the profane for the cause of God. "One finds great difficulty in uniting two forms of life," he observed one day. "One is tempted to imbalance. The difficulties are: either we live too much for ourselves or we live too much for others. The contemplative life is the soul of the active life." Writing, printing, setting type, planning out magazines, producing films or TV programs...acquired the value of a prayer, a sermon or a liturgical act. The presses were new pulpits and the distribution agencies new churches in which God's word was communicated.

To prepare men and women capable of undertaking this bold program, Father Alberione did not want to make use of any other institute with analogous apostolic ends, nor did he want to call in selected teachers (although these were not lacking) to instruct his boys. The new mission was born with great faith in God, and this faith sustained him in his resolution to shoulder the whole burden of the new task himself. He himself was to be the teacher of his boys.

Around 1930, when these had grown up and they, too, were teaching the new boys, they spontaneously began to refer to the Founder no longer as "the Theologian" (the traditional epithet) but as the *Primo Maestro*. This more comprehensive and exemplary term meant "First Teacher." "First" not only because he was the Founder but also because he was the first of all the leaders of the Institute — superiors of houses, masters of postulants and novices, heads of departments in the apostolate....

By analogy Mother Thecla became the *Prima Maestra* of the Daughters of St. Paul. This she was in a particular way. "You will have other *Prime Maestre*," the Founder told Mother Thecla's daughters after her passage to eternity (since this is the title the Congregation gives to its mother general) "but only she was above all the *mother* of the Congregation."

She made herself the pattern, the teacher of fidelity to the charism of the Founder, and annihilated herself to generate faithful followers. Her most delicate and difficult mission was that of allowing all the spirituality and light that God had given the Founder for the new family to pass through her; hers was a Marian attitude and function. As Mary "kept all these things in her heart," so Mother Thecla conserved the teachings of the Founder and immediately translated them into life for the sisters.

I repeat, it was a very difficult task, requiring an extraordinary interior life, complete self-annihilation, unreserved self-donation, perfect fidelity. Thecla Merlo was this interior masterpiece. For her, to live and act for the Founder meant to live and act for Christ; to live for her sisters was to be all to all. A true handmaid of the Lord, she gave her all so that Christ would be preached through her sisters; and in order that nothing would cloud the purity of the proclamation, she sought to the end to disappear, to conserve her function of heart rather than head, fully realizing the two points of departure and arrival of Christian, and especially Pauline, asceticism: "He must increase; I must decrease"; and, "It is no longer I who live, but it is Christ who lives in me."

Her first collaborator writes of Mother Thecla: "I would say that her whole life was based on a very simple, elementary, evangelical plan, which she followed in depth, heroically." It was St. Paul's plan of spirituality, which is the Gospel, nothing else.

Jesus Master, Way, Truth and Life is the Model to follow with the aid of "the four wheels," a name given to the spiritual bases which for Father Alberione form the total man and total Christian. These are piety, study, apostolate and poverty.

It is not difficult to sum up the entire life of Mother Thecla under these four guiding principles. She was a faithful incarnation of them.

Piety—Ancient and Modern Virtue

Among the testimonies given about Mother Thecla is that of Father Alberione himself, concise and penetrating: "This is my one general statement: for fifty years I had communication with Mother Thecla. She never failed to carry out what was planned, notwithstanding much sacrifice.... One felt that she was all of God and lived in Him.... When she became superior, her love grew. She used to say, 'If we love the Lord, let us serve Him well, doing His will with love.'"

Called to the guidance of young women launching out into a missionary adventure that was very modern and, under certain aspects, daring, at the crossroads of the world, where communications among men were incessant—Mother Thecla understood that it was her task to balance that natural centrifugal force with an incessant summons to the "one thing necessary." The more needed the apostolate, the more deep-rooted must be the spirituality. In this she gave the example, and she expected a similar deportment on the part of her sisters.

"We must build the palace of our sanctity: we are in this Congregation because the Lord has called us to become saints," she would sometimes say to the novices and professed sisters.

When these inverted the hierarchy of values, she did not hesitate to correct them: "Some do not think of prayer at all, as if it were only a duty for their sisters but not for themselves. Instead, we must love piety first of all, praying truly and fervently, not shortening the time of the hour of adoration, etc. Then love study, the apostolate and poverty." She reinforced this concept in a thousand ways, on a thousand occasions: "In our communities the most important thing is not apostolate but the practices of piety—in other words, the spirit, the interior life well lived. First we must fill our hearts with God so as to then pour out this love upon souls through the apostolate."

She instilled into her daughters a sense of what has more value: "Years pass, and thus life passes. We will not be aware of having lived, and already God will call us." Therefore, "What a misfortune to fall into lukewarmness. It would be like setting foot on a slope covered with a sheet of ice; one would slide all the way to the bottom."

And she stressed, "What are we here for, if not to become saints? We have renounced family and everything, and sometimes we live worse than seculars!"

Activism worried her: "Let us never place the apostolate first. First, we are religious, then typographers; first religious, then seamstresses; first religious, then writers; first religious, then propagators of the word."

She would also say: "One cannot have recollection during the day if she does not make her meditation. Have you ever experienced this? One becomes nervous; she sees everything distorted; she succeeds in nothing.... We need God. We must be united to Him or else we will do no good."

Mother Thecla understood that the new Congregation's strength of expansion would be multiplied only by the firmness of the roots that grounded it in God. She did not let herself be impressed by results humanly extraordinary or by the particular capabilities of one sister or another. How much had this particular daughter of hers progressed in sanctity?

Holiness was her yardstick; a Pauline's interiority was her best virtue, for with it she could accomplish the purpose of the Congregation.

"If we want the apostolate to progress," she said in a conversation in September, 1959, "our own interior life has to progress; if we want the Congregation to move ahead and establish itself well, we must be souls of deep spiritual life; there must be saints in the Congregation!"

She taught the novices a simple way of attaining to holiness: "Let us not think of the year or the

months that must pass. No, only of this day, but not
even of this day: of this hour, of this moment—for
we do not even know whether we will still be alive
an hour from now. If the present moment is sanctified,
the days and months and years of our life will be
sanctified as well."

And against openness to modern innovations
she remarked during a conversation in September,
1962, "As one goes ahead in the religious life she
can be tempted to take back something of her 'yes'
(of religious profession).... One may be tempted
...to modern innovations, thinking that some portion of what we are continually reminded about is
out-of-date and that it is better to turn to the modern
instead.... But what things are modern? The means
for doing good to mankind must be modern, but virtues are always ancient."

Writing to the sister responsible for the houses
of the United States, she stressed the formation of the
sisters, especially the novices: "If they love prayer
and pray well, they will progress; if not, their vocation
is in danger."

"Our work," she observed with profound insight, "is what saves us, but it must be animated by
union with God. I pray much for this."

"I pray for all the sisters, that we may have a
true sorrow for sins, a firm faith (the faith that moves
mountains, as Jesus says in the Gospel), a lively hope
for heaven, a burning love like that of our father,
St. Paul, a well-tried humility, an heroic obedience,
extreme poverty, a great love of common life, the max-
imum fidelity to the directives given, industriousness not to lose a minute of time, great love for the
Congregation and the apostolate, right intention that
makes us do everything for love of God, filial devotion to the most holy Virgin, who makes us her

apostles, and a holy death—death in a state of great fervor that signals a passage from this land of exile into the blessed homeland."

"Saints Are Made at the Tabernacle"

Do you recall the famous night at the beginning of the century which Father Alberione spent in prayer before the tabernacle? "Everything is born," he would say later, "from the vital font of the Eucharistic Master. Thus, from the tabernacle the Pauline family has been born; from the tabernacle it nourishes itself, lives, works and sanctifies itself. Everything—both holiness and apostolate—come from the Mass, Communion, the Eucharistic Visit." Father Alberione always spoke of the Eucharistic Master. "The Institute," he stated, "professes devotion to the Divine Master, living in the Eucharist."

Pauline spirituality has been concisely defined by one studious Pauline, Father John Roatta, as "the spirituality of human completeness and personal development under the evangelical influence of Christ the Master." This spirituality finds its entire inspiration in the Eucharist. It takes hold of the whole person, plunges him into the paschal mystery of Christ's death and resurrection, develops love, creates community, animates apostolate. Jesus gave Himself to us in the word and in the Eucharist.

Mother Thecla so lived this concept that she never neglected an opportunity to repeat it to her sisters. And there are two episodes in her life that I am tempted to relate here to show how her existence was bound to the tabernacle.

The first took place in Alba in the early days of the Congregation and is recounted by a Pauline priest, who at that time was a seminarian entrusted with the care of the chapel. "One evening around 9:30," he relates, "by the dim light of the sanctuary lamp, I saw a young woman kneeling on the floor close to the sanctuary. (At that time the Daughters of St. Paul had not yet received the religious habit.) She was gazing at the tabernacle. Her arms were open, in a gesture of supplication. I looked at her and recognized her. She was Mother Thecla."

The young cleric withdrew to his room to read and to pray the rosary, but at a certain point, about two hours later, he realized he was not going to fall asleep. Drawn by curiosity, he returned to the chapel. The scene of that praying woman had impressed him.

"Mother Thecla was still there in the same position."

Meeting her three days later, the seminarian alluded to that night, and she asked him not to speak of it. Something important had taken place during her conversation with God.

The other incident occurred near the end of her life. By this time she was in the grip of her illness and could not manage to perform her practices of piety as well as she would have wished, due to lack of strength. She mentioned this to the confessor and explained to him how she made up for it: "I am always with Jesus. I go there. I take my place in chapel. I look at the tabernacle and think, 'Jesus is there. And with Him are the Father and the Holy Spirit. The whole Trinity is there and even the Church, which is Jesus' Mystical Body—the saints and blessed of heaven, the apostles, confessors and virgins.'"

She asked the confessor whether what she had said was correct, and having received his affirmative reply, she continued, "Well, I stay there with Him, in His presence, and think this way, simply this way. Not many thoughts come to me...."

"Hers was not the simplicity of the immature," observes the priest, "but rather that of one who has reached consummate perfection, one who has drawn so close to God as to reflect His own simplicity."

The sisters still repeat to one another an incisive expression of Mother Thecla's that dates from one of the first talks she gave to the novices after her transfer to Rome: "Saints are made at the tabernacle." She often reminded her sisters of the presence of the Master: "What good fortune! What good fortune to have Jesus right here near us. When we pass by the chapel, let us try to be respectful; at least let us give a thought to Jesus, if we don't have time to pay Him a little visit."

During a special course of spiritual exercises in April, 1963, when the arc of her life was already bending towards its end, she made a comment to the sisters with regard to their hour of adoration. It was a very practical comment, revealing a straightforward religious constancy: "Suppose you close the book center early, and people come to look for you. If you do not go to serve them because you are in church making your hour of adoration, the people will understand and will be edified. They esteem us, not because we work, hurry and accomplish many things, but because we pray."

Prayer—dialogue with God. God always, before all else. This was the teaching of Mother Thecla, given life by her own exemplary consistency.

"Let Us Open the Little House of Nazareth"

For Mother Thecla, the Blessed Virgin was the "Prima Maestra" of the Congregation, the great teacher. She repeatedly said this and wrote this to her daughters. She especially wanted them to venerate Mary as the Queen of Apostles and as the woman who accomplished God's will perfectly. It was Mother Thecla's desire that the internal circular of the Daughters of St. Paul, which serves as a bond linking together all the sisters scattered throughout the world, be titled *Regina Apostolorum*—"Queen of Apostles."

To this Queen of every apostolate, Mother Thecla daily consecrated the work of her sisters. Hers was not a sentimental devotion towards the Mother of God, but a personal relationship with her who gave the world the Word: Jesus. No one ever presented Christ to the world more truly than did she who generated the whole Christ for mankind; who was made mediatrix of the Word, of the eternal Logos; who consumed her life in silence so that the living Word—Christ, the Son of God—would stand out and resound to the farthest bounds of the earth.

This profound vision of Mary's role and her natural place in Pauline spirituality gave Mother Thecla great joy. In the course of her travels, she imparted to her sisters—with a few simple strokes—an entire heritage of Marian theology. It was not fashioned of theories, but of vital experience. For example, in leaving a house she would say, "Let us open the little house of Nazareth, promising that we intend to be the little children of the Blessed Mother. Our 'Prima Maestra' is the Blessed Virgin; I leave, but she remains. Thus, the remembrance that I leave you is: be always with Mary, live with Mary, do as Mary did."

"The holy Madonna" is an expression that recurred frequently on the lips of Mother Thecla. For her, I repeat, the Mother of God was not a phantasm of religious devotion but a living being, mystically present where Jesus was continuing His work of redemption. Because of the Pauline sisters' particular tasks of service—the humble diffusion of God's word —and because of their mother general's relationship of dependence to the charism of the Founder, they mirrored the Marian features of their vocation more than the masculine branch did.

Mother Thecla strengthened this almost innate characteristic of the feminine Pauline vocation. "Let us model ourselves on the Blessed Virgin," she would say. "She kept in her heart and pondered over everything Jesus said and everything she saw Him do."

One evening, at the end of 1958, Mother Thecla suggested to the novices that they spend the new year in a "life of union" with Mary. In her skillful way of breaking the bread of the most sublime theology into small pieces for the sustenance of her sisters, she said, "Let us ask Mary to carry us in her arms, just as a mother does with a small child: for the smaller and more humble we are, the more we can remain in the arms of the Blessed Mother."

"With Mary everything is done more willingly; with one's mother everything is easier," she was accustomed to say. And in one of the last conversations that was preserved, she remarked, "The Blessed Mother has exactly this role—to make hard things easy."

Right from the beginning of the Congregation, the Marian spirit was continually cultivated by Mother Thecla.

She suggested that the sisters recite the rosary together in the car when on their way to carry out distribution. The month of May was always celebrated with particular devotion throughout the Congregation. And one of the Marian traditions of this religious family is the recitation—morning and evening—of the chaplet, "Virgin Mary, Mother of Jesus, make us saints."

Mother Thecla ardently inculcated, "May the Blessed Virgin make us saints. We ask this of her at least a hundred times a day. Truly, once and for all, may she make us saints!"

And she wrote: "Let us have great trust in the rosary recited in the month of October. Here in Rome it is said in common in the evening. See whether you, too, can do it. We recite it before Eucharistic Benediction; you arrange it as you can."

We have already mentioned the generous dedication with which Mother Thecla wished to contribute to the building of the shrine of the Queen of Apostles in Rome, to fulfill the vow made by the Founder during the Second World War. She assumed responsibility for a great part of the expenses, recommending to her daughters that they pledge themselves to collaborate in every way. To the sisters of the United States she wrote: "*Deo gratias* for your generosity! This tells me always more about your attachment to the Congregation and also to the Blessed Mother—for what you give to me is used for her shrine. Your steps are all counted! Courage! You will be remembered in this very special novena to the Immaculate Conception.... How good our Lady is!... Trust in her always more."

She studied St. Louis de Montfort's *True Devotion to the Blessed Virgin Mary*, and when she had finished she decided to consecrate herself to Mary. She also introduced the study of this book into the novitiate, suggesting that all the young sisters also make such a consecration.

She confided her worries to the Blessed Virgin.

One of her letters is quite revealing: "We have made a beautiful retreat on the theme of the Blessed Virgin. Let us consecrate everything to her. I have even consecrated our debts. Let us entrust everything to her; she is our Mother. I have great faith that she will make all of us saints."

To one of the sisters she wrote: "Be closely united to the Blessed Mother.... May she accompany you always. Love her greatly and you will become a saint—which is the most important thing."

In her eyes the sanctification of all the sisters truly was what mattered most. She asked this with faith of the Blessed Virgin at Fatima, where she stopped during a journey she made in 1949.

Mother Thecla was a soul intimately and profoundly Marian. Without this Marian hallmark, the feminine branch of the new Pauline Institute might never have reached its present-day dimensions.

Charity Before All Else

This intense life of prayer and union with God animated Mother Thecla's love of God and neighbor.

Her commitment was at once simple and heroic: "To see the will of God in all things." Whenever something was not going well, she attacked the difficulty by welcoming it rather than by enduring it: "Not resignation, but sincere, loving acceptance."

The choice of God, which is the first commitment of the religious life, cannot remain in the cloud of uncertainty. Surely it was nothing nebulous for Mother Thecla. The "yes" that she pronounced at the beginning of her adventure was truly, considering the circumstances and times, a genuine act of love of God. Even now it is difficult to understand how that physically fragile woman had been able to overcome the hardships and difficulties that a new spirituality met when incarnating itself in the ecclesial and social life of today.

For Mother Thecla, love of God showed itself even through love of contraditions, of difficulties — in a word, of the cross. She reached out for the cross instead of pushing it away. And in this she revealed a strong spirit and recalled the examples of the first women martyrs — if by martyrdom one understands, as one must, not the generous act of a moment, but an uninterrupted series of generous actions performed throughout an entire lifetime.

"Instead of carrying the cross," she observed one day, "some drag it. But then the cross bangs one's legs and causes still more suffering. We mustn't drag the cross; we must carry it."

"When we embrace the religious life, we know that this means embracing a life of sacrifice, embracing humiliations, embracing Jesus. It is useless for us to fabricate other ideas. Religious life is this way."

"I would say," she explained during the last Lent of her life — that of 1963 — "not to choose crosses for ourselves, not to ask for them, but to take the one God sends us, day by day, moment by moment. Doesn't it seem to you that we already have enough occasion to deny our will? We would like to do one thing, and we are told to do another. We would like to go to one place, and we are sent to another. We would like to continue that particular duty, and we are placed with that person we find disagreeable...."

Here we have a practical catalogue of self-renunciation, which can be translated into an authentic demonstration of charity. For Mother Thecla the religious life was this daily crucible, which consists, I repeat, in the denial of self in little things

coupled with a lively charity towards those who are
near. For, while you deny yourself, you love whomever is near you. Out of your renunciation blossoms
love. Indeed, charity shown in an ever more concrete
way towards those who are near is the most eloquent
sign of love of the cross. Common life provides a
thousand daily opportunities to test love of God and
neighbor.

The little suggestions Mother Thecla made to
the sisters were born of life-experience and a profound understanding of the souls of her daughters.
She would recall that St. John used to urge the first
Christians to love one another, to wish one another
well. "So I, too, tell you," she would say. "We must
love one another, bear with one another mutually,
sympathize with one another. Don't criticize. Don't
ridicule. Don't tease the sisters, especially those who
show that they don't care for jokes; this may even be
a lack of charity."

The illustrations continued: "Let us not expect
our sisters to be free from defects; we all have them.
We must mutually put up with one another. Let us
not excuse ourselves by saying we are nervous....
That would be meanness. We must know how to con-
trol ourselves always. Let us not grumble or answer
back or become angry with one another.... Away with
pouting, away with touchiness, away with small
grudges."

"Our houses ought to be 'little heavens,'"
Mother Thecla often declared, "just because of the
practice of charity. And together with charity, patience—patience with ourselves, with our companions and with things." And she would continue, "If
someone hears a word that displeases her a little, she
should not stop to comment on it, to report it, to mull
it over and become disgusted by it. Let's forget

ourselves a little. Let's not always concentrate on ourselves. Let's think of the others, too, a little."

Mother Thecla would suggest that her sisters always see whatever was positive around them and never think evil. For this she had recourse to a picturesque comparison: "Some people are like wasps; others, like bees. The wasps see only the evil; the bees see only the good. Let us know how to conceal the faults of the sisters and see the good." Here is a key guideline.

To a sister-superior she wrote: "You see, the sisters really have to be taken as they are. We must not expect to make them all in one image, *our own*. It is important that they be observant, yet even then we all will always have many little defects. Then, we must convince ourselves that as they grow older the sisters also have their own ideas; we can't treat them like children. I've already experienced this, and I've resolved to bring them to the Lord and that is all. Either they go this way, or they go the other way—as long as they go to Him."

Mother Thecla would also tell her sisters, "To be ready to receive a sisterly correction is also charity. Sometimes this is difficult. Yet if we investigate why we have bad humor over what has been called to our attention, we see that often it is only self-love and our ego. But has one perhaps chosen to become a Pauline to parade her self-love? We must be disposed to sacrifice anything whatsoever in order to obtain great union by charity."

To sacrifice all for charity: "It is self-love that keeps us from smiling or from speaking with a sister who has displeased us. This is not right; we must be stronger, more supernatural, looking at things from on high, not from the rooftops down."

In short, her daughters were to be a supernatural militia, a living image of that Gospel which
they were to preach by means of the press. How could
they bring God's word to others unless they made it
the cement, the bond, that held them united? Once
she reminded her sisters of what Jesus told His
disciples: "Where two or three are gathered in my
name, there am I in their midst." And she commented,
"He says, 'gathered in my name,' meaning gathered
in the name of God, and God is love." Therefore, she
concluded, "So that God will be with us, let us main-
tain charity among ourselves. It is the most important
virtue and also the most difficult."

And it is quite clear that to Mother Thecla
charity was one thing, and propriety and good manners another. Sometimes they might coincide in their
ways but never in their intentions. Propriety is a
means of making a good impression; charity, a
means of serving others. When others are in bed, one
may close doors gently or walk softly out of good
manners, but if one does it out of love, she enlivens
the community with the breath of the Holy Spirit, who
is charity.

"Make This Penance of Studying"

In Pauline spirituality, study is not the privilege of a group of qualified persons, but a daily
duty of every member, from the priest to the brother,
from the young woman to the sister. It contributes
to the integral formation of the person, who cannot
reach human fulfillment, as the Council observes,
except through the acquisition of culture. And it
contributes to the diffusion of the word. How can
one propagate and diffuse what one does not know?
Study serves the apostolate.

"The *raison d'être* of the Society of St. Paul and the Daughters of St. Paul," Mother Thecla emphasized, "is to use modern means in order to do good. Be careful not to go astray, to envy other sisters. We must perform our apostolate: films, radio, press, television and then whatever will come after...."

The mastery of the new instruments of social communication (including those "that will come after") does not call for spur-of-the-moment activity, but rather, solid study, comprising cultural and professional preparation.

Mother Thecla encouraged her sisters to acquire this training, keeping watch, however, that they would never attain it at the expense of the interior life, and that they would direct it all to the apostolate. In the end, this was the greatest undertaking among the many that Mother Thecla carried out in the course of her industrious earthly existence: she gave thousands of girls a taste for a new apostolate, at the same time preserving their religious vocation from the dangers of activism.

Women had never before been seen staffing book centers. Still less had they been seen trying their skill with a motion picture camera, with the layout of a magazine, with radio and television programs.

The vast horizons of the new apostolate, for which the course of Father Alberione's bark was set, called for considerable technical know-how. The Daughters of St. Paul had to enter into the same fields as corresponding secular undertakings. Mother Thecla was perfectly aware of the risk that all this involved, yet she had faith in success. It was such a faith as to cause her to say, "Our Congregation will always be young and will never grow old, for it will

use every new invention to do good to souls." Therefore, although the media already known required so
much time and effort, she would not refuse those to
come in the future.

It was enough for the sisters to prepare themselves with attentive study and to be able to gather
everywhere whatever was useful for their apostolate.
"It is necessary to try to study, to learn from everything, to learn every sector from the kitchen to the
book center, to exercise our intelligence continually,
so as to do well in all things."

Apostolate cannot be carried out in today's
world without knowledge. "We must always study;
our whole house is a study. I don't mean to call for
specialization, but for reflection and at least the
knowledge of how things are to be done. Be attentive
to everything, therefore, to benefit from the ad-
vances that are made in the various fields of modern
communication. It costs, to be sure. Study is an effort,
but make this penance of studying!"

Certainly, in view of the intense rhythm of life
and apostolic needs, one could never study peacefully, nor even for the amount of time truly necessary.
But the Daughters of St. Paul have not chosen to become scholars. They have chosen to love God and to
bring His word to men. "Our Congregation is based
on faith!" Mother Thecla observed forcefully. "When
one studies for an hour, she learns for four." And she
meant that God aids the learning in a special way,
in view of the time limitations within which the study
must be programmed. Certainly, however, "One
who studies must have the right intention; that is,
wanting to learn only for the glory of God and the
good of souls. Otherwise, she will not succeed." In
short, one studies for others, to serve them apos-
tolically, not for one's own personal satisfaction.

The Daughters of St. Paul must devote themselves to the necessary study, neither overrating or worshiping it, nor even neglecting it. The sisters who go out on distribution must also study, so as to be well acquainted with the content of the books they must diffuse. If salesmen know how to present their wares well, the word of God should be presented equally well and better.

The sisters assigned to film distribution must also keep updated regarding new knowledge in the field. Then there are the sisters who write. For them, "Still more than study, virtue is necessary, for then God will inspire them...." How must they write? With simplicity, explaining and popularizing the doctrine of the Church, declared Mother Thecla. And she added, "They must hold a woman's place in the Church—which is not that of the priest." Even in study Mother Thecla wanted the sisters to keep their place—a position of service, of intelligent support of the diffusion of God's word.

"The Means Used for the Apostolate Must Be the Most Modern"

"When is one an apostle?" asks Father James Alberione. "When one lives of Jesus Christ. Then one radiates Jesus Christ—radiates Him in preaching with words, in life with witness, in prayer with supplications to the Father, in deeds with productions and labor for the salvation of souls." And again: "The Pauline Congregation intends to live and give totally Jesus Christ as He was presented, lived and given to the world by St. Paul the Apostle."

We have already seen how Mother Thecla perfectly incarnated this apostolic principle of the

Founder: "One is an apostle when one lives of Jesus Christ." She could not conceive of any fruitful apostolate without interior life. Never was she overcome by apostolic activism, despite the fact that her travels in every continent had made her a sort of "confirmed traveler." Her visits to the houses scattered throughout the world constituted for the sisters as many injections of the supernatural, of more profound communion with God. Even though she showed a great practical sense and uncommon gifts of organization, it could clearly be seen that this activity of hers sprang from an interior flame that devoured her, not from a zest for accomplishment.

Nevertheless, the quantity of her achievements is impressive. But precisely from this can be measured the great apostolic anxiety of Mother Thecla. Right from the humble origins of the Congregation in Alba, she was profoundly impregnated with the universalism of St. Paul. She knew that what matters in the apostolate is not what one does—and one may even do little if one's means and talents are little—but it is rather the intention with which one works. The apostolate is not to recruit followers, to enroll people in an association, to increase the number of participants in a demonstration; the apostolate is to love the persons with whom one comes in contact, bringing them Christ with one's life. "The Lord has chosen," said Mother Thecla to her sisters, "to associate us to His own mission of salvation. But the apostolate is to be carried out well, performed with a supernatural spirit...."

That is, it can be exercised even without taking long trips, even while staying at home; rather, sometimes precisely while staying at home and, better yet, praying before the tabernacle—like St. Thérèse of the Child Jesus. "Why was she made patroness of

the missions? Because she had a great heart; she
thought of all humanity. Because she always did
God's will. Because she became a saint."

Thus were her sisters to be—like St. Thérèse
and like St. Paul—open to all the world. They were
to "feel the needs of all mankind," no matter what
their role in the Congregation.

When one reads Mother Thecla's letters and
the spontaneous talks she would give at the end of
her journeys, one remains lost in wonder at this
apostolic anxiety of hers and at the keenness of
vision with which she grasped the needs of every
nation. She explained these needs to her daughters,
so they would bring the Christian message to various
peoples in a suitable way.

Indeed, when traveling she had been able to
see firsthand how much more efficacious the word
of God is when communicated by persons of the same
place and language. Because of this, she never
ceased praying for an always greater number of
vocations in the lands where the Daughters of St. Paul
were established. "Oh," she exclaimed once, "if
only I could print sisters the way one prints books!"
Of course, she would have made them of every
nationality and race, according to the immense needs
that the love of God had made her see.

Her practical rules of action were two: "We
ourselves must arrive before evil arrives"; she
meant to refer to the new means of social communication, and: "These means must be the most modern
and effective."

Two significant events related to this subject
may fittingly be mentioned.

During Mother Thecla's journey of 1959—
thus recounts her companion of that time—she was
seriously interested in the work being done in a

small radio station of the archdiocese of Curitiba, Brazil. She grew thoughtful upon learning that many other stations would have willingly transmitted catechetical lessons and lectures recorded on tape by the Daughters of St. Paul, but that voltage differences and other technical difficulties made the realization of this seem practically unattainable.

As they were coming out of the radio station and Mother Thecla was conversing with the sisters about various things, she suddenly stopped short. "If you can't transmit the lectures and catechetical lessons on tape, make records. Records can be heard anywhere, can't they?"

Her companion was astounded, for by saying this, instead of simplifying things, Mother Thecla had complicated them. How could records be produced in Curitiba? Curitiba was not Buenos Aires or New York. Humbly the sister tried to persuade Mother Thecla to change her mind. "No, no!" was the reply. "Do it. Do it. Good has to be done. God's word has to be preached. Do it!"

Again there was an attempt to gain time: "We'll try to learn about it and do what we can."

"Do it soon," was the firm reply. And she continued, "Even if the records are not perfect in the beginning, that doesn't matter, as long as good is done. Then, little by little, you will perfect them."

The next day, on the way to the airport, the sisters pointed out a beautiful new building. "What do you think of opening a book center there?" they asked.

"Fine," came the reply. Then—just a few minutes before arriving at the airport—Mother Thecla gave her final exhortation, pinning down all of them to put their faith in what had been decided: "Make the catechetical records soon, I beg you. I am sure you will make them well and they will do good. And don't take the time to consult many people. Don't make a lot of noise. Do it right away and trust in God. He will bless you. I will pray for this."

Who could resist this apostolic logic? A few weeks later the records began to spin and to diffuse the lectures of the Paulines....

Now the record studio has been transferred to São Paulo, the great industrial and cultural metropolis of Brazil. Hundreds of catechetical, biblical, liturgical and formative titles have been cut and diffused widely throughout Brazil.

The second episode concerns Bolivia. In October, 1963, discussions were going on as to whether a house should be opened there. In fact, news and general knowledge showed that most of the inhabitants of this land were illiterate. How could the apostolate of the press be carried out, if the people did not even know how to read?

To remove the uncertainty of those in charge, Mother Thecla hammered home her nail with the usual firmness. "If the majority of the people can't read," she said, "you can do good through pictures and records. But there, too, it is necessary to open a center of apostolate. There, too, the Lord must be made known. There, too, the Gospel must be spread in some way."

Let it be noted that this was in 1963, the vigil of her passage to eternity. Until the end, Mother Thecla bore consistent witness to the meaning of: "service to the word of God."

"Broaden Your Vision
To Take in All Mankind"

So that the apostolate of her daughters would be fruitful and efficacious, Mother Thecla endeavored to infuse in them the spirit of adaptation appropriate for a Congregation that had established itself in all continents. She did nothing other than repeat to them and have them meditate what the Founder had once incisively declared when outlining the apostolic program of the feminine branch of his Institute: "The Daughters of St. Paul must have a heart and mind as vast as that of Jesus and that of St. Paul, who knew how to make himself all to all to gain all for Christ."

They must "broaden their vision to include all peoples of whatever continent, nation or region; they must ask the Lord for the knowledge of how to educate and sanctify...."

In the course of her long journeys, Mother Thecla had grasped the individuality of every nationality and, having been able to appreciate them all, she had endeavored to cultivate in her daughters a vision that was Catholic, or universal, which respected the endowments of every person and group. She was well aware that the word of God is blocked not by varying customs but by the rejection of hearts hardened by pride. "To educate means to cultivate the attitudes of nature and gifts of grace that are present in a soul.... Hence, it is not necessary to eradicate every habit and custom, but only those which are evil. Neither must natural inclinations be repressed nor languages conformed; but the religious spirit is to be infused, along with a life of faith and sacrifice, love of God and of apostolate. It is this that truly matters; everything else serves as adorn-ment."

If some custom could seem unreasonable to one's mentality, it must not be despised because of this. Rather, one must adapt oneself to the mentality of the place. If one wants to penetrate into a nation and win its people to Christ, "one must adapt to them." In a word, adaptation to the customs and even more to the characters and temperaments of indi-vidual peoples is something essential for the Daugh-ters of St. Paul. And if shortcomings are found— for every people has its defects together with its good qualities—none are to be considered of less account for this reason.

"Love, and always love for all"—this was Mother Thecla's slogan. "In love we find ways to accomplish the good that is possible to us."

In short, one could run the risk of refusing the word of God to some men on the excuse that they do not think as we do, dress as we do, speak as we do. "Let us not so restrict our mentality as to inter-change the secondary with the essential," Mother Thecla would point out. "Let us ask God to give us the grace of a universal mind and a great heart, like that of St. Paul, so we can save many souls, so we can be the educators of all."

With regard to the changing circumstances and more or less pleasant events in connection with which the apostolate must be carried out, a radical adaptation is necessary for apostolic souls. They must "adapt themselves to the times without complaining; rather, seeing everything as permitted by God."

With this, Mother Thecla showed how alert her gaze was in knowing how to understand universally the language of the daily news, which would later become history; she was contributing to the interpretation and prediction of the "signs of the times."

There is, in fact, an essential relationship between the word of God and the signs of the times.

Health, Too, Serves the Apostolate

Mother Thecla showed particular solicitude for the health of her sisters, and this concern redounded to the advantage of the entire apostolate.

She used to say that it was each one's duty to do whatever she could to keep healthy, and that the most effective means of accomplishing this is abundant nourishment. To nourish oneself is a duty like any other. There are sisters who have to be coaxed to eat; often they do not eat out of caprice or out of displeasure with what has been provided. "Few excuses!" Mother Thecla would say. "It's not so much the matter itself that counts as the consequences. One could lose her health," she observed wisely, "and thus truly lose her vocation."

Furthermore, if this vocation is the service of the Lord through the apostolate, all one's energies must be consumed for this purpose, without holding any of them back for oneself, by either "spending them only halfway or losing oneself in nonsense." Hence, there should be good health in order to have the strength to serve the Lord, and this strength is to be employed totally for Him.

"But I'm tired," someone would tell Mother Thecla.

"Naturally," she would respond. "Some ask to be 'put on pension.' We must work, giving all our energies to the Lord. In heaven, in eternity, we will rest."

Others, instead, tend to overdo it. "They don't know how to regulate themselves," Mother Thecla would say. "They have a mania for staying up at night. This isn't good. Do things with good judgment; take the necessary rest and follow the schedule."

Some were ill once and now they watch themselves to see whether by chance they are coming down with some other sickness. "But if someone was sick once she should not believe she will always be so. What is this 'profession' of calling ourselves sick? A person preoccupied over this loses time, and then 'the body that is pampered becomes a tyrant.'"

This truly admirable balance of Mother Thecla with regard to the health of her sisters must be kept in mind if one is to understand her many motherly cares and the kindness she expressed on many occasions.

She gave the superiors of the convents the particular obligation of watching over the health of the sisters. And, as has already been seen in recounting her journeys, many times Mother Thecla authorized the acquisition of a means of transportation, so that the efforts of the sisters who went out on distribution would be lightened. She desired that— insofar as was humanly possible—nothing should be lacking to her sisters nor to the maintenance of their health.

Yet she wanted them to be ready, completely dedicated to the service of the word of God. A sister's health is not for her own well-being, but to be spent for the glory of God.

The sisters still recall a phrase from the last brief conversation Mother Thecla had with a group of superiors at Grottaferrata a few months before her passage to eternity. She had wanted to go to see them. After having addressed a few words to all, she conversed with each one. And she concluded with, "Be happy. Are you well? It seems to me that someone is pale."

She, who was already very ill, said, "I need to have patience." She, who was already pale, looked at the others and said, "It seems to me that someone is pale...."

She was truly the Mother.

The "Wheel" of Poverty

Father Alberione always presented poverty, above all, as freedom: "St. Paul says that those who run in a race do not load themselves with bundles and suitcases, but wear only the necessary for the sake of speed." Poverty detaches one from the things of this world; and the more a soul is detached from the earth the richer will it be in faith, in hope, in love of God, in heavenly wisdom, in the gifts of the Spirit. In a word, it becomes rich in all, or rather in *the All*.

In the thought of Father Alberione, poverty is intimately bound up with industriousness. For him, to speak of poverty is to speak of a person's greatest activity. "When we labor, when we employ our intelligence and health in working and doing, we imitate God more.... Pauline poverty has five functions: it renounces, produces, conserves, provides and builds up."

In Mother Thecla it is not difficult to see these five functions of Pauline poverty in action. Indeed, her biography could have been structured around these five points. Certainly for her, "The observance of poverty is the foundation and wealth of the religious life and of the apostolate," as stated the constitutions to which she continually recalled her daughters.

Poverty liberates from every earthly attachment. To be poor means to be empty of all else and to be full of God. But isn't this the religious vocation — to be filled with God? Unless one is decisively resolved to renounce all, she places an obstacle to the spiritual life. In this regard Mother Thecla never had reservations and never tolerated exceptions.

"There is a way of living poverty well: place everything in common. Certainly, there are some things that one must have, because they are personal, but it is not necessary to make stockpiles.... Let us keep only the necessary and put the rest for common use."

"And what is that bad habit of throwing away old garments or using them as rags?"

"If ordinary lay people do so much in order to economize, we religious, who have the vow of poverty, must do at least as much."

I have chosen to record these little admonitions of Mother Thecla to illustrate her inflexibility regarding the fourth "wheel" of the Pauline spirituality.

She knew that when it comes to poverty the penetration of just a drop can bring about the entrance of a flood. One hole is enough to cause the entire dike of poverty to crumble. "Poverty is like a protecting wall, the sustaining wall of the Congregation; if this wall is missing, sooner or later one will fall into ruin."

And naturally the poverty of the Congregation begins with the poverty of its members. Therefore, "Let the superiors also be careful not to make unnecessary expenditures, and let the sisters be careful not to dispose of anything. Things are not ours, and we must not do with them as we please."

"And be careful, lest with the excuse of pleasing some relative, the ugly beast of nepotism may enter through the hole of compromised poverty. This hole may be...a piece of chocolate which one pockets in order to give it to a nephew; or money given to relatives so they will bring cheese, oil or some pieces of cloth; or a request to a benefactor: 'Send something to my relatives.' All these things can be done, certainly, when there is a real need, but with the permission of the superior. Someone who freely does what she wants with something is administering it, and we cannot administer. Therefore we cannot give anything to people outside the Congregation without permission, much less waste, destroy....

"Certainly we lack poverty if we do not take care of what we use, such as clothes, etc. In this regard, clothes must be very clean and neat; but if they have some patches, we must not feel ashamed.... We must be content if we have hardships and lack something.... This, too, is to accept poverty."

The Daughters of St. Paul will never lack the means of progressing in their apostolate if they live poverty. There is a cause-and-effect relationship between poverty and apostolate. The latter increases and expands in proportion to the former. "If we observe poverty," Mother Thecla counseled, "we will also have more means for carrying out the apostolate."

The apostolate with the means of social communication calls for enormous expenditures and purchases. Motion picture cameras are expensive; printing presses are expensive; all the technical equipment used in the various sectors of the Pauline apostolate is expensive.

When people see the buildings, film studios and pressrooms, they think the Paulines are rolling in money. Perhaps even some sister might think this, when she notes that her environment is always comfortable, well kept, and modern. This might especially happen to a sister who never lived through that series of difficult years at the beginning.

"Certain sisters believe we are rich," said Mother Thecla when conversing with someone in 1961. "They think the Congregation is rich. And if we did not have to keep the secret and could reveal all our debts, we would shock them."

This continual recall to detachment from all things was necessary for sisters who had to ready themselves to work closely with the most costly and modern instruments of distribution and communication and to administer money. If the spirit of poverty were to falter, what would distinguish these ranks of sisters sent forth to conquer the world? How would they differ from the ordinary manipulators of the means of social communication? Only if they have renounced everything and only if the passion for diffusing God's word had become their ideal, could the work undertaken bear fruit. "Not merchants, but apostles; not saleswomen, but sowers of the word of God." It was a refrain that Mother Thecla never tired of repeating.

The "Ora et Labora" of the New Monasteries

Because the Congregation does not live on alms and is a modern order rather than a mendicant one — can you imagine how one could buy the costly instruments of apostolate by going out to collect alms! — the work of the sisters is the source of every undertaking. Their poverty expresses itself in work. One who does not work not only steals her sister's bread, but also hinders the growth of the apostolate. Because of this, "Poverty is also observed by not losing time, by trying to make oneself useful to the Congregation, by working rather than by wandering around to chatter and even pretend to be busy, while accomplishing little or nothing." Mother Thecla inculcated in the sisters what the Founder often said—namely, those who are well must provide for more people than themselves, for a sick sister and an elderly sister as well.

Surely work costs, but as an expression of poverty and love of God it becomes truly precious. One who works with this spirit carries on apostolate, even if she works in the kitchen or sweeps the stairs. For Paulines must also perform these more humble tasks, passing from the book center, film agency or distribution, to the stove and laundry without effort or ill humor.

A Daughter of St. Paul must have the same ideal as the Apostle: to preach the Gospel with all the modern means of social communication. But to attain this ideal it is necessary to be detached from everything—therefore living poverty in full—and to love work as sacred, as a means for carrying out the work of God.

In the convents, book centers, film and television agencies of the Daughters of St. Paul in the twentieth century, the fruitfulness of the Benedictine binomial, "pray and work" is experienced in a new way. The *ora et labora* of the Pauline sisters takes its rhythm from the clicking of typewriter keys, from the cadence of printing rollers, from the crackle of moving celluloid.

But even today the meaning of this offering of prayer and work to which thousands of young people have consecrated their lives preserves the fascination of the most authentic Christian spirituality.

Mother Thecla was at once the guardian and animator of this.

The Crucible of Common Life

"The better one adheres to common life, the holier she is," declared Mother Thecla. And it is not easy to live with others, for in general we tend to isolate ourselves and not try to establish close relations with others who live under the same roof. It is not easy, because a true rapport with others must always be a charitable one. Common life is a crucible; defects stand out already, yet one is quick to publicize them. In solitude no one knows what she is really worth, because there is no possibility to make a comparison. A saint once said: "A soul who lives in charity for forty days makes more progress than he would by living in penance for forty years." Fundamentally a person who makes penance and scourges and torments himself is always concentrating on himself; instead, one who lives in charity must forget himself to serve another.

It is exactly this that takes place in common life—the forgetting of self for the service of others. Mother Thecla knew well that common life is hard, that training is needed, that one must have courage to carry it out. But Jesus said, "The violent are seizing the kingdom of God."

Mother Thecla exhorted her daughters: "Do violence to yourselves so as not to slip out of common life, not to follow the tendencies of self-love and the temptations to withdraw within yourselves, refusing to communicate with the others. We are all sisters; we must all help one another to gain merits, to carry out common life well, to keep the rule, leaving aside all 'ifs' and 'buts.' "

"To seek out the company of one's sisters and to take part in all the common activities whenever possible—this is holiness. Follow the schedule for rising and retiring; this, too, is part of common life. In short, don't take yourself out of it too easily. And one can slip away, even though she remains present physically, every time she does not wholeheartedly participate in what the other sisters are doing and saying."

"When one is a professed sister, she has greater freedom. This is also reasonable. It is supposed that one is mature and knows how to use her time well. Time is precious and not to be lost uselessly. Even if someone has a little task she would like to perform by herself during recreation time, let her bring it into the community room and stay with the others."

"Staying together is a purification of defects, the casting off of useless baggage in order to be able to advance towards holiness more quickly. What is the purpose of common life if not this? We must become saints. All the Daughters of St. Paul must become saints!"

"And they must also have a heart full of mercy and be capable of understanding and sympathizing— overlooking another's outburst of impatience, not broadcasting a sister's act of rudeness."

Mother Thecla knew that she must fuse the members of her Congregation, which was growing within the Church, into one heart and one soul. She recommended common life as a means of organizing well this new militia of the Daughters of St. Paul. The specific service that the sisters were to render in the Church called for a profound spiritual formation, readiness to help one another concretely, a strong will to reach holiness. As has been said and repeated, a Daughter of St. Paul cannot go about through the fields of apostolate without the protection of a sound interior life, and Mother Thecla acutely reckoned that this would be better cultivated through the sharing of individual experiences, difficulties and successes. In the crucible of her own convent, every Pauline can find supernatural nourishment for her own apostolic labor; by isolating herself from communion with the others, she becomes a branch detached from the vine.

And to nourish these branches extending throughout the world, Mother Thecla took upon herself an enormous burden of correspondence and travels. With farsighted activity, she herself constituted the firm bond and cement of unity of the Daughters of St. Paul, whom she kept up-to-date — either by letters or with her own living words — regarding everything taking place at the center and periphery of the Congregation. And everywhere her letters arrived, or better still where she arrived in person, community formed itself; the sisters again found themselves to be members of one and the same body. To link the sisters to one another and keep the various houses united to one another despite the distances between them and the difficulty of communicating, was the goal and also the crowning achievement of Mother Thecla.

Everywhere she went, she recalled her daughters to the essential, to mutual charity, to holiness. "Let us endeavor to make our egoism die always more

completely and to fill ourselves with God," she wrote
from New York in January, 1946.

"Every day that passes convinces me always
more that the most important thing is to love the
Lord and to do His will," she wrote the same year
from Buenos Aires. "Never even think: 'Mother
Thecla doesn't write to us; she doesn't remember us!'
No, I remember you and I carry all of you in my heart,
all of you from the oldest to the one who entered
last, even though I do not yet know her."

To such a love as this, who could refuse to
respond?

"One Who Obeys Never Makes a Mistake"

Mother Thecla was a free creature—free from
personal attachments and the conditioning of circumstances—because she had learned to "trust in
the Lord." She often repeated this phrase in difficult circumstances. Already by nature she was
surely not a woman to drown in a glass of water. But
still more, she knew how to act with sureness once
she had clearly foreseen the work God had entrusted
to her.

"She was most docile to me," Father Alberione
said of her. "In everything to be done she asked
permission. She never raised objections. She would
carry something out at once, and in the best way."
This is the very precious testimony of him who had
been able to test the daily self-giving of a creature
who wanted to be a docile instrument in God's hands
until death.

"Trusting in the Lord," Mother Thecla remained calm amid storms, traveled the new paths
required by the newness of the mission, bore with the

critics and overcame the obstacles that were in-
evitable because of the modern character of the apostolate to be performed. In a short time she had
reached the point of keeping her soul "motionless in
God." She entered often into her "cell," as St. Catherine of Siena called the interior cloister. She entered
it every time she wished, notwithstanding her intense activity. She was one of those rare souls whose
action does not harm contemplation because they
immediately relate to what has more value.

If it is true that every founder of a religious
order in the Church is a living word of an aspect of
the Gospel, and a witness to a spirituality arising
from the deposit of the revealed message, Mother
Thecla was the silence in which that living word
resounded—the silence that made the word stand
out; she was the ground of a design, the depository of
a charism. She translated fidelity to that charism into
a supernatural obedience which was not weakness
and passivity but stimulating and creative action
to incarnate in young women the plan of God entrusted to Father Alberione.

She saw the will of God in the will of Father
Alberione; she saw God who commanded before she
saw him who was God's instrument. Because of this
she made herself, too, an instrument, in an obedience
that was total, without reservation, even when she
had to overcome great stresses and sometimes
grope in the dark.

"Always see God," she once advised her
sisters. "I obey because God is in the person commanding." She wanted them to do the same, and to
see God not only in the superior but also in the
head of one's department: "It is the same thing.
In fact, if we obey someone younger, someone less

capable than ourselves, we gain more merit than we
would if we obeyed the mother general."

Hence, a supernatural obedience, carried
out for love of God, is necessary in order to be always
more docile instruments in His hands for the accomplishment of His work.

"But superiors make mistakes, too.... Yes, but
God does not make mistakes. And you have not
chosen the superiors, but God. From the beginning
you resolved to see His will in the will expressed
by them."

In an apostolic undertaking so filled with
needs, daily requiring new changes and adjust-
ments, one cannot harden herself and defend her
own private sphere, restrict her own generosity,
overvalue her own opinions. In a word, "one should
not make a nest for herself," but be like Jesus, who
never had a place to lay His head.

In an apostolic undertaking organized in every
continent for the diffusion of the word of God,
everyone must be ready to accept the responsibility
entrusted to her. How can one reply, "I don't feel
like it"? There must be so much unity that each
can replace the other.

One who through necessity is appointed to
more humble services must not feel that she has
been lowered. Tomorrow, instead, it may be her lot
to go out on distribution or to serve in the book
center. But what does it matter where one is and
what duty she is performing? What matters is to
serve the Lord, to love Him. And this means to be
the smooth, solid stone that supports the building
wherever it is placed—in the foundation as in the
walls, in the windowsill as under the beams of
the roof.

For Mother Thecla the will of God was the positive, daily, continual construction of an accomplishment He had entrusted to her. She passed from little things to the greatest with that naturalness attained by souls committed to interior perfection. She was obedient to the core and wanted her daughters to be the same. As she accepted the decisions of superiors, whatever they might be, so she wanted her sisters to accept them. And they were to accept them with serenity.

"Once," recounts a sister who was a department-head, "because of substantial difficulties in my work, I became disgusted and found it hard to accept an order. Mother Thecla, who shared greatly in my suffering (indeed, it was also hers), urged me to obey, stressing the supernatural motives. She did this gently but decisively, even though it required effort, for her eyes were filled with tears."

"Let us obey," she would repeat often.

She also said this to a community of sisters who had not been permitted to acquire a building they thought they really needed. "In recompense," she commented, "you will find a better one." After a few months her prediction came true literally.

When conversing with her daughters, Mother Thecla often held the "constitutions" in her hands and quoted them. As she was faithful in keeping the constitutions, so she wanted them kept by her daughters, because the constitutions were the will of God.

"Sometimes," she said one day, "with the excuse of working, we go and come, make arrangements and talk...all without permission.... This does not please the Lord. Before leaving the house, one must say what she is going to do. Then something unforeseen might come up, and in such a case it is enough to report it afterwards. But never withdraw yourself from obedience, because what is not done in obedience is not for God.... One who removes herself from common life without need removes herself from the life of God. The will of God is our sanctification, and we reach sanctity through the faithful practice of common life and through religious observance as required of us by the constitutions."

She would say, "The constitutions are the will of God for the religious."

"Let the most ardent *Deo gratias* burst forth from our hearts," she wrote to the community when the constitutions received final approval. "Let us rejoice, because today with the certitude that comes from the official recognition of the Church we can say: 'We are in the will of God.' The path we tread is the one that leads to the peaks of sanctity. And so that our gratitude may be more living and true," she continued, "let us reinforce it with the resolution to want to live the constitutions — to be, each one of us, 'living constitutions.'"

Mother Thecla, who had experienced changes, transfers, detachments from places and persons dear to her, urged her daughters, "not to attach the heart — neither to persons nor to the house, nor to one's duty, nor even to a particular nation." She said, "Work wholeheartedly where you have been sent, put all your heart in the task that has been given you, but always be ready to leave it, to change at any moment."

Continually she recalled them to their prime reality — Him whom they had chosen.

"I Want To Become a Saint at Any Cost"

"The *Prima Maestra* (First Teacher) was truly *first*"—so stated the Founder—"*first* in virtue, *first* in religious observance, *first* in fraternal charity."

With Mother Thecla God has truly written— and in an outstanding manner—a modern chapter in human history. This chapter is simple and profound, as the words of God Himself are simple and profound. "Those of you who knew her," testified Cardinal Cushing of Boston, "know very well that she was a contemplative soul. She lived in continual union with God. In my opinion, there is no doubt that she was a saint—an extraordinary woman, supernatural."

Said Cardinal Larraona: "One could see that she felt God—that she blended contemplation and action in a marvelous way. Contemplation became life, changed into life...a life in which all is seeing God, serving God, communicating God."

Through Mother Thecla, God has shown the people of today a new brand of holiness, among other things so adherent to the postconciliar climate that it calls for commitment in the ecclesial and human spheres with the most firmly rooted fidelity to the message of Jesus.

It is extraordinary and marvelous that a humble woman, the daughter of farm folk, while dedicating herself to the construction of a tower of interior perfection, has extended her charity outward to the farthest bounds of the world, illuminating millions of creatures with the light of the Gospel, through culture, the press, the mass media of contemporary progress.

The humble seamstress of Castagnito d'Alba challenged the modern centers of diffusion of thought

and information by collaborating in the building of
a Congregation that must use the same instruments to
spread the word of God.

With this purpose, Mother Thecla dedicated
herself to making the infant Congregation put down
strong roots. She grounded herself and her daughters
in God more completely day by day. For fifty years
she had the young plant absorb more and more from
the solid earth of interior life. She carried out a
humble and hidden task of strengthening the roots
and sustaining the generous hope of the full flowering
of the mission.

To her hope in the mission — which was
a virtue prophetic of future development — she had
also bound her hope in her own supernatural destiny.
"I want to become a saint at any cost," she wrote one
day, "only for the greater glory of God. I rely on
the Lord completely in everything. At the end of my
life, may the eternal Father give me at the heavenly
banquet whatever place He chooses."

She attained sanctity. She has reached her
place.

Appendix

The Church has taken into consideration the personal sanctity of Mother Thecla Merlo.

In fact, on October 26, 1967, a little more than three years after her death, the then Cardinal Vicar, His Eminence, Luigi Traglia, opened before the Vicariate of Rome the informative process on the reputation for sanctity, life, virtues and miracles of the *Servant of God*, Mother Thecla Merlo.

On December 10, 1968, the questioning process about the same Servant of God was opened in the diocese of Alba (Cuneo).

On June 10, 1970, the new Cardinal Vicar, His Eminence, Angelo Dell'Acqua, opened in Rome the process concerning the "non-cult" and the writings of the Servant of God.

On May 4, 1971, the questioning process in Alba was concluded.

On March 23, 1972, His Eminence, Cardinal Dell'Acqua, concluded the informative process in Rome.

With regard to the writings of Mother Thecla Merlo, the Sacred Congregation for the Causes of Saints has already made arrangements for their examination by two theological consultants, who have given their favorable vote.

Now we await the intervention of God by means of miracles worked through the intercession of the Servant of God, Mother Thecla Merlo.

For the convenience of those who wish to call upon her intercession, we add the prayers prepared for this purpose by the postulator of the cause.

PRAYER

Most Holy Trinity, we thank You for the singular gifts of light, grace, and virtue which You granted to Sister Thecla Merlo, and we thank You for having chosen and constituted her the wise mother and sure guide of the Daughters of St. Paul.

Through her intercession, grant that we may live of her great loves: Jesus Master in the Holy Eucharist, the Church, the Gospel, and souls — souls sought and served through the Apostolate of the Editions to the point of total sacrifice.

O Lord, if it be in the designs of Your divine wisdom, carry out even on this earth, for this very devoted Daughter of St. Paul, Your divine promise: "If anyone serves me, my Father will honor him." Exalt this faithful Servant, to the joy of the Church and the good of many souls, and grant us, through her intercession, the favor we ask of You.... Amen.

Glory be....

(With ecclesiastical approval)

PRAYER

Most Holy Trinity, Father, Son and Holy Spirit, we thank You for having created, redeemed and sanctified Your humble and faithful servant, Sister Thecla Merlo and for having constituted her Mother and Co-Foundress of the Daughters of St. Paul who are consecrated to the apostolate of the mass media of communication.

Deign now to glorify her even here on earth, granting us, through her intercession the grace we ask of You....

O Mary, Mother, Teacher and Queen of the Apostles, support our plea with your maternal intercession. Amen.

Glory be.... Hail Mary....

(With ecclesiastical approval)

Anyone who receives graces and favors through the intercession of Mother Thecla Merlo is asked to send this information either to:

REV. MOTHER GENERAL
FIGLIE DI S. PAOLO
Via Laurentina 289
00142 Rome, Italy

or to

REV. MOTHER PROVINCIAL
DAUGHTERS OF ST. PAUL
50 St. Paul's Ave., Boston, Ma. 02130

Daughters of St. Paul

In Massachusetts
50 St. Paul's Avenue, Boston, Mass. 02130
172 Tremont Street, Boston, Mass. 02111

In New York
78 Fort Place, Staten Island, N.Y. 10301
625 East 187th Street, Bronx, N.Y. 10458
525 Main Street, Buffalo, N.Y. 14203

In Connecticut
202 Fairfield Avenue, Bridgeport, Conn. 06603

In Ohio
2105 Ontario St. (at Prospect Ave.), Cleveland, Ohio 44115
E. Eighth Street, Cincinnati, Ohio 45202

In Pennsylvania
1127 South Broad Street, Philadelphia, Pa. 19147

In Florida
2700 Biscayne Blvd., Miami, Florida 33137

In Louisiana
4403 Veterans Memorial Blvd., Metairie,
New Orleans, La. 70002
86 Bolton Avenue, Alexandria, La. 71301

In Missouri
1001 Pine Street (at North 10th), St. Louis, Mo. 63101

In Texas
114 East Main Plaza, San Antonio, Texas 78205

In California
1570 Fifth Avenue, San Diego, Calif. 92101
278 17th Street, Oakland, Calif. 94612
46 Geary Street, San Francisco, Calif. 94108

In Canada
3022 Dufferin Street, Toronto 395, Ontario, Canada

In England
57, Kensington Church Street, London W. 8, England

In Australia
58, Abbotsford Rd., Homebush, N.S.W., Sydney 2140,
Australia

A List of Books
By Rev. James Alberione

FATHER ALBERIONE'S PRAYERBOOK

Prayers composed by this modern apostle of the media for the members of his religious congregations are now made available to everyone.

Because he lived what he thought and wrote, Fr. Alberione's dynamic spirit is transmitted through these pages—a spirit of deep communion with God in the midst of the most intense activity.

Clear and direct, these prayers open new horizons for exploration, new depths of relation with Jesus Christ, the Divine Master; Mary, Queen of the Apostles; and St. Paul the Apostle. Here is a rich spirituality which can be delved into and shared.
318 pages; $4 plastic

THE PASCHAL MYSTERY AND CHRISTIAN LIVING

This series of meditations on the passion, resurrection and ascension of the Lord Jesus aims at deepening the Christian's understanding of the central event in time—the Paschal Mystery—and that event's transcendence of time and space to permeate the lives of each of us at every moment.
200 pages; cloth $3.93; paper $2.95

WOMAN: HER INFLUENCE AND ZEAL

"Fr. James Alberione sets forth precisely what the Christian woman should be, regardless of her age or station" ("The Priest").
316 pages; cloth $3.50; paper $2.50; Magister paperback 95c

CATECHISM FOR ADULTS

New Vatican II edition updated by the Daughters of St. Paul. Beginning with the origin of things, Fr. Alberione treats of the principal problems of reason and faith, e.g., response to the Creator's love; man's destiny; the Church's teaching role, and many more topics to satisfy the modern mind's quest for eternal truths.
256 pages; paperback $1.25

LEST WE FORGET

Reflection on the deceased brings relief for those beloved souls, since it arouses us to offer prayers and sacrifices for them, and benefits us, because the thought of eternity helps us shun sin and grow in perfection.
252 pages; cloth $3; paper $2

THE SUPERIOR FOLLOWS THE MASTER

The author shows a clear and profound understanding of religious community relations and his counsel is given with depth and clarity to superiors of religious women.
214 pages; cloth $3; paper $2

CHRIST, MODEL AND REWARD OF RELIGIOUS

Practical applications of fundamental truths for those dedicated to a modern apostolate. Every chapter indicates the harmony between the essentials of a deep interior life and a dynamic apostolate.
208 pages; cloth $3

GLORIES AND VIRTUES OF MARY

A moving presentation of Mary's heroic virtues and great privileges, drawn from Sacred Scripture, patristic writings and Vatican II documents.
251 pages; cloth $3; paper $1.50

MARY, HOPE OF THE WORLD

A brilliant consideration of Mary in the Old Testament; in her earthly life as Co-redemptrix of mankind; in her life of glory in heaven, in the Church and in the hearts of the faithful.
222 pages; cloth $3; paper $1.50

MARY, MOTHER AND MODEL

The history and aim of 30 Marian feasts, their part in the Roman Breviary, and the benefits to be derived from their observance. Illustrated.
237 pages; cloth $3; paper $1.50

PERSONALITY AND CONFIGURATION WITH CHRIST

A masterful and challenging blend of psychological insight and ageless wisdom. Written in the spirit of the Second Vatican Council with emphasis placed on the importance of the person, Fr. Alberione presents a step by step process of personality development and fulfillment that culminates in the final goal of configuration with Christ, Way, Truth and Life.
192 pages; paper $2

THE LAST THINGS

Life will never look the same again when one has finished this book. Behind every event the mind's horizon envisions eternity. "A fine collection of spiritual thoughts and prayers that might well serve as a personal 'do-it-yourself' retreat" ("Today's Family").
360 pages; cloth $3.50; paper $2.50

LIVING OUR COMMITMENT

A series of meditations on the exercise of the cardinal and moral virtues in daily religious life. In accord with the conciliar spirit, they present traditional asceticism in a manner geared to our swift-paced and outgoing era.
168 pages; cloth $3; paper $2

GROWING IN PERFECT UNION

A genuinely supernatural treatment of faith, hope and charity and religious growth in these virtues.
132 pages; cloth $2.50; paper $1.50

PRAY ALWAYS

A solid and fundamental explanation of the need and value of prayer, various methods of speaking with God and the reward of closer living with God in daily life.
264 pages; cloth $3; paper $2

"The works of Father Alberione introduced me to him and his thought for the first time; I find him simple and deep and beautiful."

Canadian Bishop

Order from addresses on page 254.